DECIDE
FOR
YOURSELF

How History
Views the Bible

OTHER BOOKS BY DR. GEISLER

The Christian Ethic of Love
Ethics: Alternatives and Issues
Philosophy of Religion
The Roots of Evil
Inerrancy (general editor)
Biblical Errancy: Its Philosophical Roots (general editor)
To Understand the Bible—Look for Jesus
Christian Apologetics

DECIDE FOR YOURSELF

How History Views the Bible

Norman L. Geisler

**ZONDERVAN
PUBLISHING HOUSE** OF THE ZONDERVAN CORPORATION
GRAND RAPIDS, MICHIGAN 49506

DECIDE FOR YOURSELF: HOW HISTORY VIEWS THE BIBLE
Copyright © 1982 by The Zondervan Corporation
Grand Rapids, Michigan

First printing, February 1982

Library of Congress Cataloging in Publication Data
Geisler, Norman L.
    Decide for yourself.
        1. Bible—Evidences, authority, etc.—History of doctrines. I. Title.
BS480.G43   220.6'01   81-16083
ISBN 0-310-39301-9   AACR2

Edited by Richard P. Polcyn
Designed by Martha Bentley

Printed in the United States of America

The author wishes to acknowledge his extensive use of quoted material from the following:

The Holy Bible, the New International Version. Copyright © 1978 by New York International Bible Society. Used by permission.

G. C. Berkouwer. *Holy Scripture: Studies in Dogmatics.* Grand Rapids: Eerdmans, 1975. Used by permission.

Archibald A. Hodge and Benjamin B. Warfield. *Inspiration.* Grand Rapids: Baker Book House, 1979. Used by permission.

C. S. Lewis, *Reflections on the Psalms.* New York: Harcourt, Brace, 1958. Used by permission.

John R. Rice. *Our God-Breathed Book—the Bible.* Murfreesboro, Tenn.: Sword of the Lord, 1969. Used by permission.

Philip Schaff, ed. *Nicene and Post-Nicene Fathers,* History of the Christian Church, vol. 3. Grand Rapids: Eerdmans. Used by permission.

Contents

Preface

Who wrote the Bible? God or men? If God inspired men to write the Bible, what did He inspire? Their thoughts? Or their words as well? How far does inspiration extend? Does it include only spiritual matters, or does it also include history and science?

The contemporary battle for the Bible has the average Christian understandably confused. Actually there is more than one battle, for there are at least six views on the nature and origin of the Bible. In using labels to identify the various views of Scripture, we must be aware that such labels are not absolute in the sense that they precisely define all those who hold to one position or another. They represent the core position of each of the various categories, but there is a divergence of viewpoints within the categories, and some theologians may even hold to different elements of more than one category.

1. Most evangelicals hold the "orthodox" view (ch. 5); that is, the Bible is divinely inspired in its very words, including matters of history and science.

2. "Liberal" theologians (ch. 6), on the other hand, believe that only parts of the Bible are divine. They see great religious value in much of Scripture; but other parts are rejected as myth, and some are even considered barbaric.

3. Some "fundamentalists" (ch. 7), strongly reacting against liberals, have affirmed that the Bible was verbally dictated by God, even to the point of modern scientific precision.

4. "Neoorthodoxy" (ch. 8), another reaction to liberalism but without returning to a fully orthodox view of Scripture, holds that the Bible is not a revela-

tion from God. Rather, it is a fallible human record of the revelation God gave in His past actions. That is, God does not reveal Himself in words but only in events.

5. "Liberal-evangelicals" (ch. 9) believe that the Bible is wholly human in origin, replete with historical, scientific, and religious errors. They believe God takes these human words and "elevates" them to be a vehicle of His word.

6. Much of the contemporary debate is between the orthodox or evangelical Christians and the "Neo-evangelicals" (ch. 10). The latter believe that the Bible is infallible but not inerrant; that is, the Bible speaks with divine authority and complete truthfulness on salvation matters but is not inerrant (without error) in historical and scientific matters.

Most of the views on the origin and inspiration of the Bible claim support from the Bible and from the great teachers of the church (chs. 1–5). This is particularly true of the orthodox, fundamental, and neoevangelical views. Each claims its view is biblical and is the historic position of the church. For Christians who do not have access to the writings of the teachers of the church and who have not made a separate study of the biblical data, these overlapping claims are confusing. For this reason I have compiled this resource book of the important statements of the major representatives of these positions.

From practical considerations, it was necessary to be selective. Within the limits of a small book, I have tried to be fair and representative in the quotations presented. By a minimal use of deletions (. . .) and by descriptive headings, I have attempted to give the proper context for each author's quotations. For those who wish to read more extensively on the topic, the sources are given for all quotations.

The purpose of the introductory chapter on the Bible is to present in one location many of the biblical texts on the origin and nature of Scripture. These are the standard by which the claims of the various views are to be measured. Of course, not all verses on the topic could be included; and, admittedly, some speak only to parts of the Bible. Therefore, the reader will have to consider the verses in their context and then decide for himself how they apply to the discussion at hand. This is, after all, a discover-for-yourself book that has as its primary aim to provide the reader with basic material to use as the starting point in making an intelligent decision as to the origin and nature of the Bible.

I wish to express my appreciation to the publishers of the several works extensively quoted herein for granting permission to do so.

DECIDE FOR YOURSELF

How History Views the Bible

1

The Bible's View of the Bible

MANY VERSES HERE refer to what the prophets expressed orally and which was later put into written form. Also, some verses refer to specific parts of the existing Bible and only by extension to the whole Bible.

THE OLD TESTAMENT

I. The Origin of Scripture

A. *The Words From God*

And Aaron told them everything the LORD had said to Moses (Exod. 4:30).

Do not add to what I command you and do not subtract from it, but keep the commands of the LORD your God that I give you (Deut. 4:2).

"As for me, this is my covenant with them," says the LORD. "My Spirit who is on you, and my words that I have put in your mouth will not depart from your mouth, or from the mouths of your children, or from the mouths of their descendants from this time on and forever," says the LORD (Isa. 59:21).

"This is what the LORD says: Stand in the courtyard of the LORD's house and speak to all the people of the towns of Judah who come to worship in the house of the LORD. Tell them everything I command you; do not omit a word (Jer. 26:2).

The lion has roared—
   who will not fear?
The Sovereign LORD has spoken
   who can but prophesy?
                              (Amos 3:8)

B. *Conveyed Through Humans*

I will raise up for them a prophet like you from among their brothers; I will put my words in his mouth, and he will tell them everything I command him (Deut. 18:18).

The Spirit of the LORD spoke through me;
   his word was on my tongue.
                              (2 Sam. 23:2)

While they were bringing out the money that had been taken into the temple of the LORD, Hilkiah the priest found the Book of the Law of the LORD that had been given through Moses (2 Chron. 34:14).

They made their hearts as hard as flint and would not listen to the law or to the words that the LORD Almighty had sent by his Spirit through the earlier prophets (Zech. 7:12).

II. The Nature of Scripture

A. *Effectual*

So is my word that goes out from my mouth:

> It will not return to me empty,
>   but will accomplish what I desire
>   and achieve the purpose for which I sent it.
>
> (Isa. 55:11)

B. *Eternal*

> The grass withers and the flowers fall,
>   but the word of our God stands forever.
>
> (Isa. 40:8)

C. *The Guide for Life*

> Your word is a lamp to my feet
>   and a light for my path.
>
> (Ps. 119:105)

D. *Infallible*

> God is not a man, that he should lie,
>   nor a son of man, that he should change his mind.
> Does he speak and then not act?
>   Does he promise and not fulfill?
>
> (Num. 23:19)

> The ordinances of the LORD are sure
>   and altogether righteous.
>
> (Ps. 19:9)

E. *True*

> Your righteousness is everlasting
>   and your law is true.
>
> (Ps. 119:142)

> Yet you are near, O LORD,
>   and all your commands are true.
>
> (Ps. 119:151)

> All your words are true;
>   all your righteous laws are eternal.
>
> (Ps. 119:160)

F. *Perfect*

The law of the Lord is perfect,
    reviving the soul.
                                    (Ps. 19:7)

Who can discern his errors?
Forgive my hidden faults.
                                    (Ps. 19:12)

G. *Powerful*

"Is not my word like fire," declares the Lord, "and like a hammer that breaks a rock in pieces?" (Jer. 23:29).

H. *The Source of Wisdom*

The entrance of your words give light;
    it gives understanding to the simple.
                                    (Ps. 119:130)

I. *Trustworthy*

Every word of God is flawless;
    he is a shield to those who take refuge in him.
Do not add to his words,
    or he will rebuke you and prove you a liar.
                                    (Prov. 30:5–6)

J. *Unchanging*

Your word, O Lord, is eternal;
    it stands firm in the heavens.
                                    (Ps. 119:89)

The New Testament

I.   The Origin of Scripture

A. *The Word(s) of God*

Jesus answered, "It is written: 'Man does not live on bread alone, but on every word that comes from the mouth of God'" (Matt. 4:4).

He called them "gods," to whom the word of God came—and the Scripture cannot be broken . . . (John 10:35).

He was in the assembly in the desert, with our fathers and with the angel who spoke to him on Mount Sinai; and he received living words to pass on to us (Acts 7:38).

First of all, they have been entrusted with the very words of God (Rom. 3:2).

So, as the Holy Spirit says:
"Today, if you hear his voice. . . ."
(Heb. 3:7)

For the word of God is living and active. Sharper than any double-edged sword, it penetrates even to dividing soul and spirit, joints and marrow; it judges the thoughts and attitudes of the heart (Heb. 4:12).

B. *Inspired of God*

All Scripture is God-breathed and is useful for teaching, rebuking, correcting and training in righteousness (2 Tim. 3:16).

You must understand that no prophecy of Scripture came about by the prophet's own interpretation. For prophecy never had its origin in the will of man, but men spoke from God as they were carried along by the Holy Spirit (2 Peter 1:20–21).

C. *Conveyed Through Humans*

He said to them, "How is it then that David, speaking by the Spirit, called him 'Lord'?" (Matt. 22:43).

When they heard this, they raised their voices together in prayer to God. "Sovereign Lord," they said. . . . "You spoke by the Holy Spirit through the mouth of your servant, our father David" (Acts 4:24–25).

We speak, not in words, taught us by human wisdom
but in words taught by the Spirit, expressing spiritual
truths in spiritual words (1 Cor. 2:13).

II. The Nature of Scripture

A. *Authoritative*

1. Absolute

   Jesus said to him, "Away from me, Satan! For it is
   written: 'Worship the Lord your God, and serve
   him only'" (Matt. 4:10).

   If anybody thinks he is a prophet or spiritually
   gifted, let him acknowledge that what I am writing
   to you is the Lord's command (1 Cor. 14:37).

   But even if we or an angel from heaven should
   preach a gospel other than the one we preached to
   you, let him be eternally condemned! . . . I want
   you to know, brothers, that the gospel I preached
   is not something that man made up. I did not receive it from any man, nor was I taught it; rather, I
   received it by revelation from Jesus Christ (Gal.
   1:8, 11–12).

   You know what instructions we gave you by the
   authority of the Lord Jesus (1 Thess. 4:2).

2. Prophetic and apostolic

   In the past God spoke to our forefathers through
   the prophets at many times and in various ways,
   but in these last days he has spoken to us by his
   Son, whom he appointed heir of all things, and
   through whom he made the universe (Heb. 1:1–2).

   How shall we escape if we ignore such a great
   salvation? This salvation, which was first announced by the Lord, was confirmed to us by
   those who heard him. God also testified to it by

signs, wonders and various miracles, and gifts of the Holy Spirit distributed according to his will (Heb. 2:3–4).

3. Timeless

Heaven and earth will pass away, but my words will never pass away (Matt. 24:35).

B. *Complete*

I warn everyone who hears the words of the prophecy of this book: If anyone adds anything to them, God will add to him the plagues described in this book. And if anyone takes words away from this book of prophecy, God will take away from him his share in the tree of life and in the holy city, which are described in this book (Rev. 22:18–19).

C. *Effectual*

Jesus replied, "You are in error because you do not know the Scriptures or the power of God" (Matt. 22:29).

"But how then would the Scriptures be fulfilled that say it must happen in this way?" (Matt. 26:54).

D. *The Foundation of Faith*

[You are] built on the foundation of the apostles and prophets, with Christ Jesus himself as the chief cornerstone (Eph. 2:20).

E. *The Guide for Faith*

But when he, the Spirit of truth, comes, he will guide you into all truth. He will not speak on his own; he will speak only what he hears, and he will tell you what is yet to come (John 16:13).

F. *Historically True*

For as Jonah was three days and three nights in the belly of a huge fish, so the Son of Man will be three days and three nights in the heart of the earth (Matt. 12:40).

Haven't you read . . . that at the beginning the Creator "made them male and female?" (Matt. 19:4).

As it was in the days of Noah, so it will be at the coming of the Son of Man. For in the days before the flood, people were eating and drinking, marrying and giving in marriage, up to the day Noah entered the ark; and they knew nothing about what would happen until the flood came and took them all away (Matt. 24:37–39).

For man did not come from woman, but woman from man; neither was man created for woman, but woman for man (1 Cor. 11:8–9).

For Adam was formed first, then Eve (1 Tim. 2:13).

G. *Indestructible*

Do not think that I have come to abolish the Law or the Prophets; I have not come to abolish them but to fulfill them. I tell you the truth, until heaven and earth disappear, not the smallest letter, not the least stroke of a pen, will by any means disappear from the Law until everything is accomplished (Matt. 5:17–18).

Jesus answered them, "Is it not written in your Law, 'I have said you are gods'? If he called them 'gods,' to whom the word of God came—and the Scripture cannot be broken . . ." (John 10:34–35).

H. *Absolute Truth*

Sanctify them by the truth; your word is truth (John 17:17).

III. The Extent of Biblical Authority

A. *To All That Is Written*

All Scripture is God-breathed and is useful for teaching, rebuking, correcting and training in righteousness (2 Tim. 3:16).

B. *To the Very Words*

Jesus answered, "It is written: 'Man does not live by bread alone, but on every word that comes from the mouth of God.'" (Matt. 4:4).

We speak, not in words taught us by human wisdom but in words taught by the Spirit (1 Cor. 2:13).

C. *To the Smallest Parts of Words*

Do not think that I have come to abolish the Law or the Prophets; I have not come to abolish them but to fulfill them. I tell you the truth, until heaven and earth disappear, not the smallest letter, not the least stroke of a pen, will by any means disappear from the Law until everything is accomplished (Matt. 5:17–18).

D. *To Verb Tenses*

Jesus replied, "You are in error because you do not know the Scriptures or the power of God. . . . Have you not read what God said to you, 'I *am* the God of Abraham, the God of Isaac, and the God of Jacob'?" (Matt. 22:29, 31–32, italics mine).

E. *To Number (singular or plural)*

The promises were spoken to Abraham and to his seed. The Scripture does not say "and to seeds," meaning many people, but "and to your seed," meaning one person, who is Christ (Gal. 3:16).

Summary

The Bible claims for itself that every word or part of a word, with tenses and number, is absolutely true since it is given by the Holy Spirit from the mouth of God, who cannot lie (Titus 1:2; Heb. 6:18). Therefore, it has final divine authority in whatever it teaches, whether it be historical, scientific, or spiritual matters. This applies to both the Old Testament and the New Testament.

2

The
Early Fathers' View
of the Bible

Bᴇᴛᴡᴇᴇɴ ᴛʜᴇ ᴛɪᴍᴇ of Christ and the Reformers
there were many important teachers in the Christian
church. These men are called "church fathers." Their
views on the Bible provide us with the historical view
of the church on the origin and nature of the Bible. The
early fathers flourished in the second and third centuries.

Cʟᴇᴍᴇɴᴛ ᴏꜰ Rᴏᴍᴇ (ᴀ.ᴅ. 30–100)

I. The Origin of Scripture: The Words of God

Let us act accordingly to that which is written (for the
Holy Spirit saith, "Let not the wise man glory in his
wisdom") (Jer. 9:23) (*First Epistle of Clement to the Corinthians* 13).

For He Himself by the Holy Ghost thus addresses us:
"Come, ye children, hearken unto me" (Ps. 34:11) (ibid.,
22).

Look carefully into the Scriptures, which are the true utterances of the Holy Spirit (ibid., 45).

II. The Nature of Scripture: Infallible

Observe that nothing of an unjust or counterfeit [false] character is written in them (ibid.).

JUSTIN MARTYR (100–165)

I. The Origin of Scripture

A. *Words From God*

But when you hear the utterances of the prophets spoken as it were personally, you must not suppose that they are spoken by the inspired men themselves but by the divine Word who moves them *(First Apology 36)*.

We must not suppose that the language proceeds from the men who are inspired, but from the divine Word which moves them. Their work is to announce that which the Holy Spirit, descending upon them, purposes, through them, to teach those who wish to learn the true religion (ibid.).

To him [Moses] did God communicate that divine and prophetic gift . . . and then after him the rest of the prophets. . . . These we assert to have been our teachers, who use nothing from their own human conception, but from the gift vouchsafed to them by God alone *Justin's Hortatory Oration to the Greeks 8)*.

B. *Conveyed Through Humans*

For neither by nature nor by human conception is it possible for men to know the things so great and divine, but the gift which then descended from above upon the holy men who had no need of rhetorical art, nor of uttering anything in a contentious or quarrelsome manner, but to present themselves pure to the energy of the Divine Spirit, in order that the Divine plectrum itself, descending from heaven and using righteous men as an instrument like a harp or a lyre, might reveal to us a knowledge of things divine and heavenly. Wherefore, as if with one mouth and one tongue, they have in succession and in harmony with one another taught us both concerning God, and the creation of the world, and the formation of man, and concerning the immorality of the human soul, and judgment which is to be after this life, and concerning all things which it is needful for us to know, and thus in divers times and places have afforded us the divine instruction (ibid., 8).

II. The Nature of Scripture

A. *Inspired in Written Form*

[Moses] wrote in the Hebrew character by the divine inspiration (ibid., 12).

B. *Inspired in Spoken Form*

And the Holy Spirit of prophecy taught us this, telling us by Moses that God spoke thus (ibid., 44).

IRENAEUS (SECOND CENTURY)

I. The Origin of Scripture

A. *The Words of God*

The Scriptures are indeed perfect, since they were spoken by the Word of God [Christ] and His Spirit (*Against Heresies* 2.28.2).

B. *Words From God*

I shall plainly set forth from these divine Scriptures proofs to [satisfy] all lovers of truth (ibid., 2.35.4).

II. The Nature of Scripture

A. *The Foundation of Faith*

The Scriptures [are the] ground and pillar of our faith (ibid., 3.1.1).

B. *Infallible*

Let us revert to the Scriptural proof furnished by those apostles who did also write the Gospel. . . . The writings of those apostles, . . . being the disciples of truth, are above all falsehood (ibid., 3.5.1).

[Heretics] adduce an unspeakable number of apocryphal and spurious writings which they themselves have forged, to bewilder minds of foolish men, and of such as are ignorant of the Scriptures of truth (ibid., 1.20.1).

We should leave things of that nature to God who created us, being most properly assured that the Scriptures are indeed perfect, since they were spoken by the Word of God and His Spirit (ibid., 2.28.2).

TERTULLIAN (ca. 160–225)

I. The Nature of Scripture

A. *Authoritative*

In granting indulgence, he [Paul] alleges the advice of a prudent man; in enjoining continence, he affirms the advice of the Holy Spirit. Follow the admonition which has divinity for its patron. It is true that believers likewise "have the Spirit of God;" but not all believers are apostles. When, then, he who had called himself a "believer," added thereafter that he "had the Spirit of God," which no one would doubt even in the case of an (ordinary) believer; his reason for saying so was, that he might re-assert for himself apostolic dignity. . . . Apostles have the Holy Spirit properly, who have Him fully, in the operations of prophecy. . . . Thus he attached the Holy Spirit's authority to that form [of advice] to which he willed us rather to attend; and forthwith it became not an *advice* of the Holy Spirit, but, in consideration of His majesty, a *precept* (*On Exhortation to Chastity* 4, italics his).

B. *Divine*

We are united. . . . Divine Scripture has made us concorporate; the very letters are our glue (*On Modesty* 5).

C. *Harmonious*

From apostolic word descends the Church,
All filled, to wash off filth, and vivify
Dead fates. The Gospel, four in number, one.
            (*Reply to Marcion* 2.70)

D. *Timeless*

No enunciation of the Holy Spirit ought to be [confined] to the subject immediately in hand merely, and not applied and carried out with a view to *every* occasion to which its application is useful (*On the Apparel of Women* 2.2, italics his).

ORIGEN (211–32)

I. The Origin of Scripture

A. *Inspired of God*

This just and good God, the Father of our Lord Jesus Christ, Himself gave the law, and the prophets, and the Gospels, being also the God of the apostles and of the Old and New Testaments (*De Principiis* preface. 4).

Therefore we shall endeavour, so far as our moderate capacity will permit, to point out to those who believe

the holy Scriptures to be no human compositions, but
to be written by inspiration of the Holy Spirit (ibid.,
4.1.9).

B. *Conveyed Through Humans*

That this Spirit inspired each one of the saints,
whether prophets or apostles; and that there was not
one Spirit in the men of the old dispensation, and
another in those who were inspired at the advent
of Christ, is most clearly taught throughout the
Churches (ibid., preface. 4).

II. The Nature of Scripture

A. *Divine*

That this testimony may produce a sure and un-
hesitating belief, either with regard to what we have
still to advance, or to what has been already stated, it
seems necessary to show, in the first place, that the
Scriptures themselves are divine, i.e., were inspired
by the Spirit of God (ibid., 4.1.1).

We take in addition, for the proof of our statements,
testimonies from what are believed by us to be divine
writings, viz., from that which is called the Old Testament, and that which is styled the New, and endeavour by reason to confirm our faith; and as we
have not yet spoken of the Scriptures as divine, come
and let us, as if by way of an epitome, treat of a few
points respecting them, laying down those reasons
which lead us to regard them as divine writings
(ibid.).

B. *Supernatural*

But if in every part of the Scriptures the superhuman
element of thought does not seem to present itself to
the uninstructed, that is not all wonderful; for, with
respect to the works of that providence which em-

braces the whole world, some show with the utmost
clearness that they are works of providence, while
others are so concealed as to seem to furnish ground
for unbelief with respect to that God who orders all
things with unspeakable skill and power (ibid.,
4.1.7).

C. *Sacred*

And was there no motive which induced them to class
with the books of Moses, which were held as sacred,
the words of those persons who were afterwards
deemed to be prophets? (*Against Celsus* 3.2).[1]

D. *True*

And in this way he might become a sharer in the
knowledge of the Spirit, and a partaker in the divine
counsel, because the soul cannot come to the perfec-
tion of knowledge otherwise than by inspiration of
the truth of the divine wisdom (*De Principiis* 6.1.14).

E. *Largely Historical*

Let no one, however, entertain the suspicion that we
do not believe any history in Scripture to be real,
because we suspect certain events related in it not to
have taken place; or that no precepts of the law are to
be taken literally, because we consider certain of
them, in which either the nature or possibility of the
case so requires, incapable of being observed; or that
we do not believe those predictions which were
written of the Saviour to have been fulfilled in a man-

---

[1]Of course, Origen was not interested in mere words but in the meaning
of these words. He wrote:

Let every one, then, who cares for truth, be little concerned about words
and language, seeing that in every nation there prevails a different usage
of speech; but let him rather direct his attention to the meaning conveyed
by the words, than to the nature of the words that convey the meaning,
especially in matters of such importance and difficulty (*De Principiis*
4.1.27).

ner palpable to the senses; or that His commandments are not to be literally obeyed. We have therefore to state in answer, since we are manifestly so of
opinion, that the truth of the history may and ought
to be preserved in the majority of instances (ibid.,
4.19).

F. *Mosaic Authorship of the Law*

Now it is probable that, from these illustrations,
those will entertain no doubt with respect to the five
books of Moses, who have once given in their adhe-
sion to the apostle, as divinely inspired; but do you
wish to know, with regard to the rest of the history, if
it also happened as a pattern? (ibid., 4.1.14).

III. The Interpretation of Scripture

A. *Not Entirely Literal*

The attentive reader may notice in the Gospels innumerable other passages like these; so that he will
be convinced that in the histories that are literally
recorded, circumstances that did not occur are in-
serted. And if we come to the legislation of Moses,
many of the laws manifest the irrationality, and
others the impossibility, of their literal observance
(ibid., 4.1.16–17).

B. *Figurative and Allegorical*

So neither is the divinity of Scripture, which extends
to the whole of it, [lost] on account of the inability of
our weakness to discover in every expression the
hidden splendour of the doctrines veiled in common
and unattractive phraseology (ibid., 4.1.7).

No one, I think, can doubt that the statement that
God walked in the afternoon in paradise, and that
Adam lay hid under a tree, is related figuratively in
Scripture, that some mystical meaning may be indi-

cated by it. . . . And what need is there to say more, since those who are not altogether blind can collect countless instances of a similar kind recorded as having occurred, but which did not literally take place? Nay, the Gospels themselves are filled with the same kind of narratives; e.g., the devil leading Jesus up into a high mountain, in order to show him from thence the kingdoms of the whole world, and the glory of them (ibid., 4.1.16).[2]

CLEMENT OF ALEXANDRIA (ca. 150–215)

I. The Origin of Scripture

A. *Commands of the Holy Spirit*

In fact, they stitch together a multitude of lies and figments, that they may appear acting in accordance with reason in not admitting the Scriptures. So, then, they are not pious, inasmuch as they are not pleased with the divine commands, that is, with the Holy Spirit (*Stromata* 7.21).

B. *Derived From God*

For God is the cause of all good things; but of some primarily, as of the Old and the New Testament; and of others by consequence, as philosophy (ibid., 5.5).

Now such to us are the Scriptures of the Lord, which gave birth to the truth and continue virgin, in the concealment of the mysteries of the truth (ibid., 7.16).

C. *The Voice of God*

But we, who have heard by the Scriptures that self-determining choice and refusal have been given by the Lord to men, rest in the infallible criterion of

---

[2]Origen's interpretations were later condemned as heretical by the church. Most scholars recognize that Origen's heretical views were due to the influence of platonic philosophy on his thinking.

faith, manifesting a willing spirit, since we have chosen life and believe God through His voice (ibid., 2.4).

II. The Nature of Scripture

A. *Divine*

The divine Scripture accordingly says, that those who
have transgressed the commandments are sold to
strangers, that is, to sins alien to nature, till they return and repent (ibid., 2.4).

Those are slothful who, having it in their own power
to provide themselves with proper proofs for the . . .
Scriptures from the Scriptures themselves, select only
what contributes to their own pleasures (ibid., 7.16).

B. *The Rule of Truth*

For those who make the greatest attempts must fail in
things of the highest importance; unless, receiving
the truth itself the rule of the truth, they cleave to the
truth. But such people, in consequence of falling
away from the right path, err in most individual
points; as you might expect from not having the fa-
culty for judging of what is true and false, strictly
trained to select what is essential. For if they had,
they would have obeyed the Scriptures (ibid.).

Summary

The earliest fathers of the church believed that the
Bible is the infallible rule for faith. It is absolutely true
in all its utterances, since it is given by God Himself.
The Bible is harmonious, containing no contradictions;
and it has absolute divine authority. This applies to all
the historical statements of Scripture as well as the
spiritual and moral truths. And with the exception of
Origen's heretical allegorizing, these fathers understood the Bible literally.

3

The Medieval Fathers' View of the Bible

THE TWO GREATEST Christian teachers in the Middle Ages stand at either end of it. At the beginning of this era was Augustine, the bishop of Hippo; at the end was Thomas Aquinas. The lesser teachers of this period held essentially the same view of Scripture.

AUGUSTINE (354–430)

I. The Origin of Scripture

A. *Inspired of God*

Among these Prophets was the one who announced in writing: "In the beginning God created the heavens and the earth." And it was so fitting that faith in God should come through such a witness that he was inspired by the same Spirit of God, who had revealed these truths to him to predict, far in advance, our own future faith (*Confessions* 11.4).

[All the books of the Bible] breathe the Spirit of ful-

ness, and there is nothing, whether in the Law or in
the Prophets, in the Evangelists, or in the Apostles,
which does not descend from the fulness of the Divine Majesty. . . . [There is not even] one jot or tittle
written in the Scriptures which does not work its own
work, when men know how to employ it (*Homily on
Jeremiah* 21.2; 39).

So too we conceive of all that has been recorded by
the inspiration of the Holy Ghost . . . [who] has
placed, so to speak, the seeds of saving truth in each
letter as far as possible (*Commentary on the Psalms*
1.4).

B. *The Oracles of God*

[He speaks of those Christian teachers] who wrote
from the divine oracles (*City of God* 10.1).

C. *The Words From God*

When they write that He has taught and said, it
should not be asserted that He did not write it, since
the members only put down what they had come to
know at the dictation [*dictis*] of the Head. Therefore,
whatever He wanted us to read concerning His words
and deeds, He commanded the disciples, His hands,
to write. Hence, one cannot but receive what he reads
in the Gospels, though written by the disciples, as
though it were written by the very hand of the Lord
Himself (*Harmony of the Gospels* 1.35.54).

II. The Nature of Scripture

A. *Authoritative*

1. An apostolic authority

   The authority of these books has come down to us
   from the Apostles . . . [and] claims the submission
   of every faithful and pious mind (*Against Faustus*
   11.5).

The truth of the divine Scriptures has been received into the canonical summit of authority, for
this reason—that they are commended for the
building up of our faith not by anybody you
please, but by the apostles themselves (*Letters*
82.7).

2. A uniform authority

Even though both quotations were not from the
writings of one apostle—though one were from
Paul and the other from Peter, or Isaiah, or any
other apostle or prophet—such is the equality of
canonical authority that it would not be allowable
to doubt either. For the utterances of Scripture,
harmonious as if from the mouth of one man,
commend themselves to the belief of the most accurate and clear-sighted piety and demand for
their discovery and confirmation the calmest intelligence and most ingenious research (*Against
Faustus* 11.5–6).

3. A unique authority

In innumerable books that have been written lat-
terly we may sometimes find the same truth as in
Scripture, but there is not the same authority.
Scripture has a sacredness peculiar to itself (ibid.,
115.5).

B. *Divine*

[He refers to] all those catholic expounders of the divine Scriptures, both Old and New (*On the Trinity*
1.4.7).

C. *Historical*

God did not even wish to create the woman who was
to be mated with man in the same way that He crea-

ted man but, rather, out of him, in order that the whole human race might be derived entirely from one single individual. . . . He took a bone from the man's side and made it a mate to collaborate in procreation. Of course, all this was done in a divine way. . . . If some people take these true facts for mere fables it is because they use familiar, everyday craftsmanship to measure that power and wisdom of God which not merely can but does produce even seeds without seeds. . . . God, then, formed man out of the dust of the earth and, by His breath, gave man a soul such as I have described (*City of God* 12.22–24).

D. *Infallible and Inerrant*

For it seems to me that most disastrous consequences must follow upon our believing that anything false is found in the sacred books: that is to say, that the men by whom the Scripture has been given to us and committed to writing, did put down in these books anything false. . . . For if you once admit into such a high sanctuary of authority one false statement as made in the way of duty, there will not be left a single sentence of those books which, if appearing to any one difficult in practice or hard to believe, may not by the same fatal rule be explained away, as a statement in which, intentionally, and under a sense of duty, the author declared what was not true (*Letters* 23.3.3).

Manifestly, therefore, Peter was truly converted, and Paul has given a true narrative of the event, unless, by the admission of a falsehood here, the authority of the Holy Scriptures given for the faith of all coming generations is to be made wholly uncertain and wavering. For it is neither possible nor suitable to state within the compass of a letter how great and how utterly evil must be the consequences of such a concession (ibid., 40.3.5).

> For I confess to your Charity that I have learned to yield this respect and honour only to the canonical books of Scripture: of these alone do I most firmly believe that the authors were completely free from error. And if in these writings I am perplexed by anything which appears to me opposed to truth, I do not hesitate to suppose that either the manuscript is faulty, or the translator has not caught the meaning of what was said, or I myself have failed to understand it (ibid., 82.1.3).

> If we are perplexed by an apparent contradiction in Scripture, it is not allowable to say, the author of this book is mistaken; but either the manuscript is faulty, or the translation is wrong, or you have misunderstood (*Against Faustus* 11.5).

THOMAS AQUINAS (ca. 1225–74)

I. The Origin of Scripture

A. *A Revelation From God*

> It was necessary for man's salvation that there be a certain doctrine according to divine revelation, truths which exceed human reason. Even regarding those truths which human reason can investigate it was necessary that man be taught by divine revelation. For the truth about God which is learned through reason would be known only by a few after a long time and with an admixture of errors; but the salvation of man depends upon his knowledge of this truth which is in God. Therefore, in order that salvation might the easier be brought to man and be more certain, it was necessary that men be instructed concerning divine matters through divine revelation (*Summa Theologica* 1.1.1).

B. *Authored by God*

That God is the author of Scripture should be acknowledged (ibid., 1.1.10).

II. The Nature of Scripture

A. *Authoritative*

We are bound to believe all the contents of sacred Scripture (ibid., 1.6.1).

B. *Infallible and Inerrant*

For our faith rests upon the revelation given to the apostles and prophets who wrote the canonical books, and not on revelation (if there be such a thing) made to other teachers. Whence Augustine says in his letter to Jerome (82): "Only to those books which are called canonical have I learned to give honor so that I believe most firmly that no author in these books made any error in writing" (ibid., 1.1.8).

It is heretical to say that any falsehood whatever is contained either in the Gospels or in any canonical Scripture (*In Job* 13. Lect. 1).

Summary

The medieval fathers of the church held firmly to the divine origin of Scripture. They believed that there could not possibly be even one error in Scripture. Any supposed error in our translation must be understood to be apparent, not real, or else to be an error in the copy but not the original. The canon of Scripture was given by God and has thereby full divine authority.

4

The Reformers' View of the Bible

DESPITE THE FACT that the Reformers reacted against many of the teachings and practices of the Roman Catholic church, they strongly affirmed the same view of the inspiration of Scripture held down through the centuries.

MARTIN LUTHER (1483–1546)

I. The Origin of Scripture

A. *The Word of God*

This is exactly as it is with God. His word is so much like himself, that the godhead is wholly in it, and he who has the word has the whole godhead (J. Pelikan and H. T. Lehman, eds., *Luther's Works*, 55 vols. [Philadelphia: Muhlenberg and Fortress, 1960], 52:46).

It must be observed, however, that another one is the author of this book [Genesis], namely the Holy

Ghost. . . . The Holy Spirit wanted to write this [Gen. 26:19–21] to teach us (M. Reu, *Luther and the Scriptures* [Columbus, Ohio: Wartburg, 1944], p. 35).

In the exposition of the Second Epistle of St. Peter, of the same year, is the statement: "Says Peter, what has been written and proclaimed in the Prophets has not been imagined nor invented by men, but holy and devout men have spoken it *through the Holy Ghost*" (ibid., p. 33, italics his).

He is called a prophet who has received his understanding directly from God without further intervention, *into whose mouth the Holy Ghost has given the words*. For He (the Spirit) is the source, and they have no other authority than God (ibid., italics his).

Here (II Samuel 23:2, "The Spirit of the Lord spake by me, and His word was in my tongue") it becomes too marvelous and soars too high for me. . . . It is these and similar statements to which St. Peter refers in the II Epistle 1:21, "For the prophecy came not in old time by the will of men, etc. . . ." Therefore we sing in the Creed, concerning the Holy Ghost, "Who spake by the Prophets." So *we refer all of Scripture to the Holy Ghost*" (ibid., pp. 36–37, italics his).

We must know what we believe, namely what God's Word says, not what the pope or the saintly fathers believe or say. For you must not rely on a person. No, you must rely on the Word of God alone (Pelikan and Lehman, *Works*, 30:105).

Would to God that my exposition and that of all doctors might perish and each Christian himself make the Scriptures and God's pure word his norm. You can tell by my verbosity how immeasurably different God's words are in comparison with any human word, how no single man is able to fathom sufficiently any one word of God and expound it with many words (ibid., 52:286).

B. *The Words From God*

And the Scriptures, although they too are written by men, are neither of men nor from men but from God. Now since Scriptures and the doctrines of men are contrary one to the other, the one must lie and the other be true (ibid., 35:153).

They do not believe they are God's words. *For if they believe they were God's words they would not call them poor, miserable words but would regard such words and titles as greater than the whole world and would fear and tremble before them as before God himself. For whoever despises a single word of God does not regard any as important,* (Reu, *The Scriptures*, p. 32, italics his).

I see that Scripture is consonant in all and through all and agrees with itself in such a measure that it is impossible to doubt the truth and certainty of such a weighty matter in any detail (ibid., p. 37, italics his).

II. The Nature of Scripture

A. *Authoritative*

We hope that everyone will agree with the decisions that the doctrines of men must be forsaken and the Scriptures retained. For they will neither desire nor be able to keep both, since the two cannot be reconciled and are by nature necessarily opposed to one another, like fire and water, like heaven and earth (Pelikan and Lehman, *Works*, 35:153).

We do not condemn the doctrines of men just because they are the doctrines of men, for we would gladly put up with them. But we condemn them because they are contrary to the gospel and the Scriptures (ibid.).

I have learned to ascribe this honor (namely the infallibility) only to books which are termed canonical, so that I confidently believe that not one of their authors erred (Reu, *The Scriptures*, p. 17).

Nothing but God's Word alone should be preached in Christendom. The reason for this is no other, as we have said, than this, that a Word must be proclaimed that remains eternally—a Word through which souls may be saved and may live forever (Pelikan and Lehman, *Works*, 30:167).

B. *Infallible and Inerrant*

Neither does it help them to assert that at all other points they have a high and noble regard for God's words and the entire gospel, except in this matter. My friend, God's Word is God's Word; this point does not require much haggling! When one blasphemously gives the lie to God in a single word, or says it is a minor matter if God is blasphemed or called a liar, one blasphemes the entire God and makes light of all blasphemy (ibid., 37:26).

So the Holy Ghost has had to bear the blame of not being able to speak correctly but that like a drunkard or a fool He jumbles the whole and uses wild, strange words and phrases. But it is our fault that we have not understood the language nor the style of the prophets. It cannot be otherwise, because the Holy Ghost is wise and also makes the prophets wise. But one who is wise must be able to speak correctly; that never fails. But because whoever does not hear well or does not know the language well may think he speaks ill because he hears or understands scarcely half the words (Reu, *The Scriptures*, p. 44, italics his).

And whoever is so bold that he ventures to accuse God of fraud and deception *in a single word* and does so willfully again and again after he has been warned and instructed once or twice will likewise certainly venture to accuse God of fraud and deception in all His words. Therefore it is true absolutely and without exception, *that everything is believed or nothing is believed.* The Holy Ghost does not suffer Himself to be separated or divided so that He should teach and cause to be believed one doctrine rightly and another falsely (ibid., p. 33, italics his).

This is a rather unimportant story, therefore we shall not devote much time to its explanation; indeed, I do not know how to say much about it. But since it is *written by the Holy Spirit,* we cannot well pass by this text but will treat it to some extent (ibid., p. 35, italics his).

C. *The Revelation of Christ*

Therefore dismiss your own opinions and feelings, and think of the Scriptures as the loftiest and noblest of holy things, as the richest of mines which can never be sufficiently explored, in order that you may find that divine wisdom which God here lays before you in such simple guise as to quench all pride. Here you will find the swaddling clothes and the manger in which Christ lies, and to which the angel points the shepherds [Luke 2:12]. Simple and lowly are these swaddling clothes, but dear is the treasure, Christ, who lies in them (Pelikan and Lehman, *Works,* 35:236).

D. *Scientifically Authoritative*

There was mention of a certain new astronomer who wanted to prove that the earth moves and not the sky, the sun, and the moon. This would be as if somebody were riding on a cart or in a ship and imagined that he was standing still while the earth and the trees were moving. [Luther remarked,] "So it goes now. Whoever wants to be clever must agree with nothing that others esteem. He must do something of his own. This is what that fellow does who wishes to turn the whole of astronomy upside down. Even in these things that are thrown into disorder I believe the Holy Scriptures, for Joshua commanded the sun to stand still and not the earth [Josh. 10:12] (*Table Talk* June 4, 1539).

Because we are not sufficiently able to understand how these days occurred nor why God wished to observe such distinctions of times, *we shall rather admit our ignorance than attempt to twist the words unnecessarily into an unnatural meaning.* As far, therefore, as St. Augustine's opinion is concerned, we hold that Moses spoke literally not allegorically or figuratively, that is, the world and all its creatures was created within the six days as the words declare. Because we are not able to comprehend we shall remain disciples and leave the instructorship to the Holy Ghost (Reu, *The Scriptures,* p. 51, italics his).

E. *Self-consistent*

Though this Epistle of St. James was rejected by the ancients, I praise it and regard it as a good book, because it sets up no doctrine of men and lays great stress upon God's law. But to state my own opinion about it, though without injury to anyone, I consider that it is not the writing of any apostle. My reasons are as follows:

First: Flatly in contradiction to St. Paul and all the rest of Scripture it ascribes righteousness to works and says that Abraham was justified by his works in that he offered his son Isaac, though St. Paul, on the contrary, teaches, in Romans 4, that Abraham was justified without works, by faith alone, before he offered his son and proves it by Moses in Genesis 15. . . .

Second: Its purpose is to teach Christians, and in all its teaching it does not once mention the Passion, the Resurrection, or the Spirit of Christ (ibid., p. 24).

JOHN CALVIN (1509–64)

I. The Origin of Scripture

A. *The Words From God*

The Bible has come down to us from the mouth of God (*Institutes* 1.18.4).

We owe to Scripture the same reverence which we owe to God; because it has proceeded from Him alone, and has nothing belonging to man mixed with it. . . . The Law and the prophets are not a doctrine delivered according to the will and pleasure of men, but dictated by the Holy Spirit (John Urquhart, *Inspiration and Accuracy of the Holy Scriptures* [London: Marshall, 1895], pp. 129–30).

Our faith in doctrine is not established until we have a perfect conviction that God is its author. Hence, the highest proof of Scripture is uniformly taken from the character of him whose word it is. . . . If, then, we would consult most effectually for our consciences, and save them from being driven about in a whirl of uncertainty, from wavering, and even stumbling at the smallest obstacle, our conviction of the truth of Scripture must be derived from a higher source than human conjectures, judgments, or reasons; namely, the secret testimony of the Spirit. . . . if they are not possessed of shameless effrontery, they will be compelled to confess that the Scripture exhibits clear evidence of its being spoken by God, and, consequently, of its containing his heavenly doctrine. We shall see a little farther on, that the volume of sacred Scripture very far surpasses all other writings. Nay, if we look at it with clear eyes and unbiassed judgment, it will forthwith present itself with a divine majesty which will subdue our presumptuous opposition, and force us to do it homage (*Institutes* 1.7.4).

The Scriptures are the only records in which God has been pleased to consign his truth to perpetual remembrance, the full authority which they ought to possess with the faithful is not recognized, unless they are believed to have come from heaven, as directly as if God had been heard giving utterance to them (ibid., 1.7.1).

But as the Lord was pleased that doctrine should exist in a clearer and more ample form, the better to satisfy weak consciences, he commanded the prophecies also to be committed to writing, and to be held part of his word. To these at the same time were added historical details, which are the composition of prophets, but dictated by the Holy Spirit (ibid., 4.8.6).

B. *Conveyed Through Humans*

As I have observed, there is this difference between the apostles and their successors, they were sure and authentic amanuenses of the Holy Spirit; and, therefore, their writings are to be regarded as the oracles of God, whereas others have no other office than to teach what is delivered and sealed in the holy Scriptures (ibid., 4.8.9).

II. The Nature of Scripture

A. *Authoritative*

For our wisdom ought to consist in embracing with gentle docility, and without any exceptions, all that is delivered in the sacred Scriptures (ibid., 1.18.4).

B. *Inerrant in the Original Manuscripts*

[Scripture is] the certain and unerring rule (*Calvin's Commentaries* Ps. 5:11).

For if we reflect how prone the human mind is to lapse into forgetfulness of God, how readily inclined to every kind of error, how bent every now and then on devising new and fictitious religions, it will be easy to understand how necessary it was to make such a depository of doctrine as would secure it from either perishing by the neglect, vanishing away amid the errors, or being corrupted by the presumptuous audacity of men (*Institutes* 1.6.3).

So long as your mind entertains any misgivings as to the certainty of the word of God, its authority will be weak and dubious, or rather will have no authority at all. Nor is it sufficient to believe that God is true, and cannot lie or deceive, unless you feel firmly persuaded that every word which proceeds from him is sacred, inviolable truth (ibid., 3.2.6).

C. *Copyist Errors*

How the name of Jeremiah crept in [the manuscripts at Matt. 27:9], I confess that I do not know, nor do I give myself much trouble to inquire. The passage itself plainly shows that the name of Jeremiah has been put down by mistake, instead of Zechariah (*Calvin's Commentaries* Matt. 27:9).

Summary

Luther was emphatic about the Bible: It is God's Word, not man's. God is the author of every word of Scripture. Absolute divine authority extends to even the smallest part of Scripture, including those references to history and science. Whoever denies anything in the Bible denies God Himself.

Calvin believed the sacred Scriptures were the unerring norm for the Christian faith. As such they deserved the same reverence as God Himself, for they originated from the very mouth of God by the dictates of the Holy Spirit. This is true not only of spiritual matters but also of the historical and scientific teachings of the Bible. The only errors were copyists' errors in some manuscripts, not in the originals.

5

The Orthodox View of the Bible

THE BEST REPRESENTATIVES of the modern orthodox view of Scripture are the old Princeton scholars A. A. Hodge and B. B. Warfield. Their view has become normative for most orthodox or conservative Christians since their time. (Note: All quotes are from A. A. Hodge and B. B. Warfield, *Inspiration* [1881; paperback reprint ed., Grand Rapids: Baker, 1979], used by permission.)

I. The Origin of Scripture

A. *The Word of God*

The New-Testament writers continually assert of the Scriptures of the Old Testament, and of the several books which constitute it, that they ARE THE WORD OF GOD. What their writers said God said (p. 29, emphasis theirs).

B. *The Words of God*

Infallible thought must be definite thought, and definite thought implies words. But if God could have rendered the thoughts of the apostles regarding doctrine and duty infallibly correct without words, and then left them to convey it to us in their own language, we should be left to precisely that amount of certainty for the foundation of our faith as is guaranteed by the natural competency of the human authors, and neither more nor less. There would be no divine guarantee whatever. . . . Whatever discrepancies or other human limitations may attach to the sacred record, *the line* (of inspired or not inspired, of infallible or fallible) *can never rationally be drawn between the thoughts and the words of Scripture* (pp. 22–23, italics theirs).

C. *Infallible*

Every element of Scripture, whether doctrine or history, of which God has guaranteed the infallibility, must be infallible in its verbal expression (p. 21).

It would assuredly appear that . . . if error be found in any one element or in any class of statements, certainty as to any portion could rise no higher than belongs to that exercise of human reason to which it will be left to discriminate the infallible from the fallible (p. 35).

The presuppositions [of inspiration] are—1. The possibility of supernatural interference, and the actual occurrence of that interference in the origin of our Bible; and, 2. The authenticity, genuineness and historical credibility of the records included in our Bible. The added supposition is—3. The truth to fact of every statement in the Scriptures. No objection from the side of criticism is relevant unless it traverses some one of these three points (p. 37).

D. *Conveyed Through Humans*

We do not deny an everywhere-present human element in the Scriptures. No mark of the effect of this human element, therefore—in style of thought or wording—can be urged against inspiration unless it can be shown to result in untruth (p. 42).

God's continued work of superintendence, by which, his providential, gracious and supernatural contributions having been presupposed, he presided over the sacred writers in their entire work of writing, with the design and effect of rendering that writing an errorless record of the matters he designed them to communicate (p. 17).

Holy Scripture was the result of the co-operation, in various ways, of the agency of men and the agency of God. The human agency, both in the histories out of which the Scriptures sprang, and in their immediate composition and inscription, is everywhere apparent, and gives substance and form to the entire collection of writings. It is not merely in the matter of verbal expression or literary composition that the personal idiosyncracies of each author are freely manifested by the untrammeled play of all his faculties, but the very substance of what they write is evidently for the most part the product of their own mental and spiritual activities (p. 12).

In all this process, except in a small element of prophecy, it is evident that as the sacred writers were free and active in their thinking and in the expression of their thoughts, so they were conscious of what they were doing, of what their words meant, and of the design of their utterance. Yet, even then, it is no less evident that they all, like other free instruments of Providence, "builded better than they knew" (p. 17).

It is evident that the stricter view, which denies the existence of errors, discrepancies or inaccurate statements in Scripture, has the presumption in its favor, and that the *onus probandi* rests upon the advocates of the other view (p. 34).

E. *Self-consistent*

But when we begin to examine the instances brought forward in support of it (i.e., alleged contradictions in the Bible), they are found to be cases of *difficult*, not of *impossible*, harmony. And it is abundantly plain that it must be shown to be *impossible* to harmonize any two statements on any natural supposition before they can be asserted to be inconsistent. This is a recognized principle of historical investigation, and it is the only reasonable principle possible, unless we are prepared to assert that the two statements necessarily contain all the facts of the case and exclude the possibility of the harmonizing supposition (p. 54, italics theirs).

F. *Historically True*

The general conformableness of the sacred books to modern knowledge in all these departments is purely miraculous. If these books, which originated in an obscure province of the ancient world, be compared with the most enlightened cosmogonies or philosophies or histories of the same or immediately subsequent centuries, their comparative freedom even from apparent error is amazing (p. 30).

G. *Scientifically True*

The first two chapters of Genesis, rightly interpreted, of itself demonstrates that a supernatural intelligence must have directed the writing of those chapters. This, of course, proves that the scientific element of

Scripture, as well as the doctrinal, was within the scope of inspiration (p. 31).

H. *Not Mechanically Dictated*

Each sacred writer was by God specially formed, endowed, educated, providentially conditioned, and then supplied with knowledge naturally, supernaturally or spiritually conveyed, so that he, and he alone, could, and freely would, produce his allotted part. Thus God predetermined all the matter and form of the several books largely by the formation and training of the several authors, as an organist determines the character of his music as much when he builds his organ and when he tunes his pipes as when he plays his keys. Each writer also is put providentially at the very point of view in the general progress of revelation to which his part assigns him (pp. 14–15).

And there is the more excuse for this misapprehension because of the extremely mechanical conceptions of inspiration maintained by many former advocates of this term "verbal." This view, however, we repudiate as earnestly as any of those who object to the language in question. At the present time the advocates of the strictest doctrine of inspiration in insisting that it is verbal do not mean that in any way the thoughts were inspired by means of the words, but simply that the divine superintendence, which we call inspiration, extended to the verbal expression of the thoughts of the sacred writers, as well as to the thoughts themselves, and that hence the Bible, considered as a record, an utterance in words of a divine revelation, is the word of God to us (p. 19).

II. The Nature of Scripture

A. *Plenary Inspiration*

Is it proper to call this inspiration "plenary"? This

word, which has often been made the occasion of
strife, is in itself indefinite, and its use contributes
nothing either to the precision or the emphasis of the
definition. The word means simply "full," "complete," perfectly adequate for the attainment of the
end designed, whatever that might have been. There
ought not to be on any side any hesitancy to affirm
this of the books of the Bible (p. 18).

B. *Verbal Inspiration*

Verbal inspiration . . . does not hold that what the
sacred writers *do not* affirm is infallibly true, but only
that what *they do affirm* is infallibly true (p. 80, italics
theirs).

C. *Inerrant*

And throughout the whole of his work the Holy Spirit
was present, causing his energies to flow into the
spontaneous exercises of the writer's faculties, ele-
vating and directing where need be, and everywhere securing the errorless expression in language
of the thought designed by God. This last element
is what we call "Inspiration" (p. 17).

We do not assert that the common text, but only that
the original autographic text, was inspired. No
"error" can be asserted, therefore, which cannot be
proved to have been aboriginal in the text (p. 42).

In view of all the facts known to us, we affirm that a
candid inspection of all the ascertained phenomena of
the original text of Scripture will leave unmodified the
ancient faith of the Church. In all their real affirma-
tions these books are without error (p. 27).

III. Criticism of Scripture

It is evident . . . that every supposed conclusion of critical investigation which denies the apostolic origin of a

New Testament book or the truth of any part of Christ's testimony in relation to the Old Testament and its contents, or which is consistent with the absolute truthfulness of any affirmation of any book so authenticated, must be inconsistent with the true doctrine of inspiration (pp. 24–25).

The present writers . . . admit freely that the traditional belief as to the dates and origin of the several books may be brought into question without involving any doubt as to their inspiration, yet confidently affirm that any theories of the origin or authorship of any book of either Testament which ascribe to them a purely naturalistic genesis, or dates or authors inconsistent with either their own natural claims or the assertions of other Scripture, are plainly inconsistent with the doctrine of inspiration taught by the Church (p. 39).

Summary

The orthodox position is that the Bible is the infallible and inerrant Word of God in the original manuscripts. It is without error in everything it affirms. Indeed, what the Bible says, God says. This includes matters of history, science, the authorship and dates of biblical books, and any other matters. Any results of higher criticism that are contrary to this are incompatible with the inspiration of Scripture and are, thereby, unorthodox.

6

The Liberal View of the Bible

THERE ARE VARYING degrees of theological liberalism. A moderate and widely read representative of the liberal perspective is the Methodist theologian Harold DeWolfe. The more radical form of liberalism is represented by Harry Emerson Fosdick.

HAROLD DEWOLFE (1905--)

I. The Origin of Scripture

A. *Not the Word of God*

Strictly speaking, the Bible itself is not the pure Word of God. Although by a figure of intimate association we may, on occasion, without impropriety, call the Bible the Word of God, we ought not to use this language in careful theological discourse (Harold De-Wolfe, *The Case for Theology in Liberal Perspectives* [Philadelphia: Westminster, 1959], p. 17).

B. *From Fallible Humans*

It is evident that the Bible is a collection of intensely human documents. These books were written by men who had their own characteristic education, interests, vocabularies and literary styles. Most of the events described are activities of obviously fallible human beings. Many passages contradict one another or well-established knowledge. Many of the moral and religious ideas, especially in the more ancient documents, are distinctly sub-Christian (Harold DeWolfe, *A Theology of the Living Church* [New York: Harper & Brothers, 1953], p. 73).

C. *The Meaning of Inspiration*

This doctrine is that the writing of the Bible as a whole was accomplished by an extraordinary stimulation and elevation of the powers of men who devoutly yielded themselves to God's will and sought, often with success unparalleled elsewhere, to convey truth useful to the salvation of men and of nations. This was possible mainly because they had truth of such extraordinary importance to convey. It is upon that truth that we must lay our principal stress (ibid., p. 76).

The human fallibility of the Bible does not preclude the possibility of its divine inspiration nor of its unmatched moral and religious authority. Although written by men with characteristic individual traits and typical human failings it may still have been written by men seized and impelled by the spirit of God (ibid., p. 75).

II. The Nature of Scripture

A. *Authority*

The authority of the Bible is not such as to be

strengthened by isolation from all other authority. Throughout the history of Christendom, Christian scholars have organized total views of the world in which the sciences, philosophical inferences from the evidences of common human experience, and the teachings of the Bible have all been woven together in unity (*Liberal Perspectives*, p. 57).

Jesus himself challenged some commands of the Old Testament. (Matt. 5:21–48) (ibid., p. 48).

But while we are treating the fallibility of the Scriptures we must note that Jesus unhesitatingly and repeatedly sets Old Testament teaching at naught (*Living Church*, p. 73).

B. *Cultural Accommodation*

Some degree of accommodation to culture seems inevitable unless Christian teaching is to become a mere irrelevant echoing of ancient creeds—which were themselves products of some accommodation to Hellenic thought (*Liberal Perspectives*, p. 58).

C. *Errant and Fallible*

To the intelligent student who is more concerned with seeking out and declaring the truth than with maintaining a dogma it must be apparent that the Bible is by no means infallible (*Living Church*, p. 68).

In regard to many facts of minor importance there are obvious contradictions within the Bible. For example, in Exodus 37:1–9 we read that Bezaleel made the Ark of the Covenant, while in Deuteronomy 10:1–5 Moses reports that God commanded him to make the Ark and he says, "So I made an ark of acacia wood. . . ." When Joab was ordered to take a census, 2 Samuel 24:1 tells us that it was by God's command while 1 Chronicles 21:1 says it was by Satan's command (ibid., p. 69).

III. Criticism of Scripture

   A. *Corrections to the Text*

The correcting of the text and the historical locating of the writing are but different aspects of one great task. The intimate and inseparable relation between textual and historical studies of the Bible seems not to be adequately appreciated by some conservative scholars. . . . Textual and historical criticism are intricately interwoven with each other and with non-Biblical archaeological, historical, and linquistic studies (*Liberal Perspectives*, pp. 51–52).

   B. *Rationalism*

Natural theology serves to correct some of the errors produced by an exclusively Biblical or by Biblical and traditional theology (ibid., p. 32).

God's word spoken to us through the Bible depends for the clarity and purity of its reception both upon our own open and understanding minds and also upon the reception and expression given his word by the ancient men who wrote the words of the Bible (ibid.).

The insistence of some conservative Christians on a Biblical literalism that is rationally indefensible and an appeal based on the "proofs" of prophecy and miracles, in defiance of the natural sciences and the new historical understanding of Biblical times, needlessly drives from the Christian faith intelligent young people who will not blind themselves to scientific and historical evidences (ibid., p. 43).

The untrained reader does well to read for the nurture of his spirit and not to become unduly concerned about passages that appear to contradict the spirit of Christ or the scientific knowledge of our times (ibid., p. 48).

C. *Scientific Errors*

Plainly the narrator [of Gen. 30:35–43] simply accepted the false science prevalent in his day.

Similarly, some or all Biblical writers assume the fixity of the earth, the actual movement of sun and moon from east to west, a space above the firmament reserved for God's dwelling and the demonological explanation of disease. Such views cannot be intelligently accepted as infallible teaching (*Living Church,* p. 71).

D. *Antisupernaturalism*

The questions whether such miracles have actually happened and if so how they should be thought of in relation to the natural order are questions needing to be considered later. Just now we are concerned simply to point out that, in the light of our theistic evidences, if a miracle were to be properly called a special revelation it could not be so-called because of its being any more an act of God than are the ordinary processes of nature, but only because it was more revealingly meaningful to men (ibid., p. 66).

HARRY EMERSON FOSDICK (1878–1969)

I.   The Nature of Scripture—Fallible and Errant

Obviously, any idea of inspiration which implies equal value in the teachings of Scripture, or inerrancy in its statements, or conclusive infallibility in its ideas, is irreconcilable with such facts as this book presents. The inspirations of God fortunately have not been thus stereotyped and mechanical (Harry Emerson Fosdick, *A Guide to Understanding the Bible* [New York: Harper & Brothers, 1938], p. xiv).

II. Criticism of Scripture

A. *Documentary Hypothesis*

This passage [Exod. 6:2–3] appears in the late Priestly document and all the more because of that the probabilities favor its truth. Without a solid basis in historic fact, such a delayed beginning of Yahweh's worship would not have been invented by succeeding generations (ibid. p. 1).

B. *Ethics*

The utmost cruelty was not only allowed but commanded by Yahweh against Israel's rivals, and in the presence of habitual conflict fine ideals of humaneness had their chance to develop only within the circle of blood-brotherhood (ibid., p. 100).

The fact that one Biblical book is later in time than another is in itself not the slightest indication that it is superior in quality—Nahum is on a much lower spiritual level than Amos, and the Book of Revelation in the New Testament is morally inferior to the writings of the Great Isaiah in the Old Testament. . . . There is no smooth and even ascent in the Book. There are, instead, long detours, recrudescences of primitivism, lost ethical gains, and lapses in spiritual insight. There are even vehement denials of nascent truth, and high visions that ~~so~~ neglected for centuries (ibid., p. xiii).

C. *Evolution*

As for the modern scene with its contemporary problems, the New Testament's idea of man faces immense difficulties in maintaining itself. The vast enlargement of the physical cosmos, the evolutionary origin of man, materialistic theories which endeavor to explain him, brutality of social life involving low conceptions of him, the innumerable masses of men such that old cynicisms gain new force . . . tend in many minds to undo what the Hebrew-Christian development did (ibid., p. 97).

On the one side we are paying for it in multitudes of churches waiting to be swamped by theological obscurantism, fanatical premillennialists, anti-evolutionary propaganda, or any other kind of reactionary movement in religious thinking against which no intellectual dikes ever have been raised by thoroughgoing consistent teaching as to what our new knowledge really means to religion. On the other side we are paying for it in the loss of our more intelligent young people (Harry Emerson Fosdick, *Modern Use of the Bible* [New York: Association, 1926], p. 61).

D. *Inconsistent*

For one thing, we are saved by it [biblical criticism] from the old and impossible attempt to harmonize the Bible with itself, to make it speak with unanimous voice, to resolve its conflicts and contradictions into a strained and artificial unity. How could one suppose that such internal harmony ever could be achieved between writings so vital and real, springing hot out of the life of the generations that gave them being, and extending in their composition over at least twelve hundred years? (ibid., pp. 24–25).

No straightforward dealing with these and other similar facts can resolve their incompatibility into even the semblance of consistent narrative. Moreover, underlying such disharmonies is the still more substantial conflict, which we earlier noted, between two ideas of Jesus' resurrected body, one altogether fleshly, the other so spiritualized as to escape the trammels of a material organism (*Guide to Understanding*, p. 294).

E. *Progressive Truth of the Bible*

   1. Cosmology

      It all was made in six days, each with a morning
      and an evening, a short and measurable time be-
      fore. This is the world-view of the Bible. . . .
      Moreover, it remained the world-view of the
      Christian church for a long time. Augustine, with
      uncompromising strictness, stated the authority of
      Scripture in matters such as this: "Scripture,
      which proves the truth of its historical statements
      by the accomplishment of its prophecies, gives no
      false information." Those early fathers have been
      severely handled because they thus clung to a
      world-view which might have been outgrown
      long before it was, had not their literalism barred
      the way. In this insistence upon an old cosmology,
      however, they were but children of their age
      (*Modern Use*, p. 47).

      Even Luther called Copernicus a fool for suggest-
      ing that the earth moved, and roundly capped his
      argument by calling to witness the Scripture
      which says that Joshua made the sun stand still
      and not the earth (ibid., p. 50).

   2. Inspiration

      Our ideas of the method of inspiration have
      changed; verbal dictation, inerrant manuscripts,
      uniformity of doctrine between 1000 B.C. and 70
      A.D.—all such ideas have become incredible in
      the face of the facts (ibid., pp. 30–31).

      The first results of critical research into the Bible
      seemed disruptive, tearing the once unified Book
      into many disparate and often contradictory docu-
      ments. The final result has turned out to be construc-
      tive, putting the Bible together again, not indeed

on the old basis of a level, infallible inspiration, but on the factually demonstrable basis of a coherent development (*Guide to Understanding*, p. ix).

3. Miracles

   Multitudes of people, so far from being well-stabilized traditionalists, are all at sea in their religious thinking. If ever they were drilled in older uses of the Bible they have rebelled against them. Get back to the nub of their difficulty and you find it in Biblical categories which they no longer believe—miracles, demons, fiat creation, apocalyptic hopes, eternal hell, or ethical conscience (*Modern Use*, p. 5).

4. Morality

   The Old Testament exhibits many attitudes indulged in by men and ascribed to God which represents early stages in a great development, and it is alike intellectually ruinous and morally debilitating to endeavor to harmonize those early ideals with the revelations of the great prophets and the Gospels. Rather, the method of Jesus is obviously applicable: "It was said to them of old time . . . but I say unto you" (ibid., p. 27).

5. Theology

   It is impossible that a Book written two to three thousand years ago should be used in the twentieth century A.D. without having some of its forms of thought and speech translated into modern categories. When, therefore, a man says, I believe in the immortality of the soul but not in the resurrection of the flesh, I believe in the victory of God on earth but not in the physical return of Jesus, I believe in the reality of sin and evil but not in the visitation of demons, I believe in the nearness and friendship of the divine Spirit but I do not think of that experience in terms of individual angels, only superficial dogmatism can deny that that man believes the Bible (ibid., p. 29).

The Book is not a good forest to cut timber in for theistic dogmatism. Not only are its ideas of God in constant process of change, but it is everywhere conscious of depth beyond depth in the divine nature, uncomprehended and incomprehensible (*Guide to Understanding*, p. 53).

F. *The Basis for Determining Truth in the Bible*

1. Human reason

   The man who ministers . . . must have an intelligible way of handling the Bible. He must have gone through the searching criticism to which the last few generations have subjected the Scriptures and be able to understand and enter into the negations that have resulted. Not blinking any of the facts, he must have come out with a positive, reasonable, fruitful attitude toward the Book. Only so can he be of service in resolving the doubts of multitudes of folk to-day (*Modern Use,* pp. 5–6).

2. Human experience

   The liberal emphasis rests upon experience; we regard that, rather than mental formulas, as the permanent continuum of the Gospel; we proclaim our freedom from bondage to the mental formulas of the past; and often the total result is that our unformulated religious experience, refusing the discipline of older thinking and shirking the discipline of new thinking, lands in chaos. It is often much easier to discover what liberals do not think than to discover what they do think (ibid., p. 183).

3. The Spirit of Christ

> So long as a man knows the whole road and judges every step of it by the spirit of Christ, who is its climax, he can use it all (ibid. p. 30).

Summary

The liberal view of Scripture is that the Bible is not the Word of God as such but merely *contains* the Word of God. Along with the truths of God in the Bible are many errors of science and theology that must be weeded out by use of reason in accord with "the spirit of Christ." Hence, higher criticism of the Bible is not only welcome but essential to discovering what is true in the Bible. Along with the rejection of much of what the Bible teaches is an antisupernaturalism that rejects the miracles of the Bible. The Bible is basically a fallible human book that contains, nonetheless, "inspired" insight into moral and religious truths.

Postscript

Fosdick had some serious second thoughts about his view of Scripture. Here is what he wrote a generation later:

> Today, however, looking back over forty years of ministry, I see an outstanding difference between then and now with regard to what is standard and who must do the adjusting. What man in his senses can now call our modern civilization standard? It is not Christ's message that needs to be accommodated to this mad scene; it is this mad scene into which our civilization has collapsed that needs to be judged and saved by Christ's message. This is the most significant change distinguishing the beginning of my ministry from now. Then we were trying to accom-

modate Christ to our scientific civilization; now we face
the desperate need of accommodating our scientific civilization to Christ (Henry Emerson Fosdick, *A Great Time to
Be Alive* [New York: Harper Brothers, 1944], pp. 201–2).

7

A
Fundamentalist View
of the Bible

ONE OF THE MOST systematic treatments by a fundamentalist is that of John R. Rice. (Not all who call themselves "fundamentalists," however, agree with Rice. In fact, perhaps most of them accept the orthodox view of Hodge and Warfield.) While no fundamentalist scholar claims to hold to *mechanical* dictation, Rice does confess his belief in the "verbal dictation" of the whole Bible. (All quotations are from John R. Rice, *Our God-Breathed Book—The Bible* [Murfreesboro, Tenn.: Sword of the Lord, 1969]. Used by permission.)

I. The Origin of Scripture

A. *Inspired of God*

    1. The Book, not the writers

        First Peter 1:10–12 is a charming and enlightening passage about how the Bible claims to speak from God so that even those who wrote did not understand what they wrote down (p. 61).

69

When we say that the Bible is inspired, we do not refer to the translations or copies but to the original autographs, written down under God's direction (p. 68).

Let us say plainly, then, that the Scriptures did not come, in any degree, from a heightening of men's natural faculties nor by common illumination to understand spiritual truth. Let us remember that inspiration refers to the Book, not to the men who wrote it (p. 75).

Yes, Christianity requires a miraculously given, divine Scripture because it is a miracle religion (p. 76).

2. God-breathed

All Scripture is "God-breathed," that is, the Scripture itself is breathed out from God. God is its origin. The miracle of the Scriptures came directly from God. . . . This is about as strong a statement as human language could make about the inspiration of the Bible. The Scripture was breathed out by God (pp. 49–50).

No, it was not men inspired but words inspired, or rather, breathed out by God (p. 71).

Let us make sure that we do not water down this express statement of Scripture about inspiration. It is not what God breathed on certain men or that they wrote and God breathed on the writings. Rather, the very words of Scripture themselves are breathed out from God (p. 52).

3. No mechanical dictation

The Bible does not teach a mechanical inspiration without using people and oftentimes their thoughts and feelings or devotions or prayers, and revealing their thoughts. The words are God's words and the Scripture is the Word of God, but it comes through men. And I do not know of a single book on the subject, or a single reputable Bible teacher or preacher who holds that despised "mechanical view of inspiration" (p. 267).

4. Uniform inspiration

That does not mean that all Scripture is as important in some particular situation as some particular part is. It does not mean that John 3:16, for example, is not to be treasured more than some narrative verse in a minor prophet. But it means that every bit of the Word of God is inspired perfectly and alike. There are no degrees of inspiration. Many evangelicals have been misled on this matter (p. 96).

5. Verbal and plenary inspiration

Bernard Ramm, no more orthodox than Orr and less theologically reliable, says that the Bible has minor errors of fact. His book is reviewed in great detail in our book, *Earnestly Contending for the Faith,* chapter 9, "Shall We Appease Unbelieving Scholars?" Ramm says, "In that inspiration came through the mold of the Hebrew culture, the hyperorthodox is wrong." By the hyperorthodox people he means those of us who believe in verbal or plenary inspiration (p. 86).

B. *By Verbal Dictation*

But this charge of "mechanical dictation" against fundamental Bible believers is dishonest pretense. The Bible never teaches that it was mechanically dictated, that is, that those who put down the words of Scripture were unconscious, that their own minds and hearts were never involved, as if God did not use men at all in writing the Bible. I say, the Bible does not teach that and as far as I know, no intelligent Christian in the world believes anything of the kind (p. 265).

Is the word *dictation* hateful? Then liberals and infidels made it hateful. Men too anxious to disavow the straw man of "mechanical dictation" have avoided and feared the term. . . . Griffith Thomas' book is labeled, *God Spoke All These Words*. And that quotation from Exodus 20:1, referring to the words of the Ten Commandments, is really a proper name for a book about the inspiration of the Bible. Well, if God gave all the words in the Bible, then is not that dictation? (p. 286, italics his).

"Dictation," says someone, "dishonors the men who wrote the Bible." Shame! Shame! So you want big prophets and a little God, do you? You do not want a man simply hearing what God says and writing it down, do you? Well, then, your attitude is simply the carnal attitude of the unbelieving world that always wants to give man credit instead of God, whether for salvation or inspiration. A secretary is not ashamed to take dictation from man. Why should a prophet be ashamed to take dictation from God?

Face it honestly, if God gave the very words and men wrote them down, that is dictation. It was not *mechanical* dictation (p. 287, italics his).

C. *Conveyed Through Humans*

   1. More than a witness

      The Bible is not composed of what men have seen, it is not the report of witnesses. The Bible is not what people have heard as they were told by others (p. 57).

      It is obviously clear that God used men. But it is

equally clear that He gave them the very words. If God saw no contradiction, if God did not feel the need to hedge and trim on this question, why should we? Why should we try to put into this plan that men copied down oral tradition or from ancient records or from their memories or from eyewitnesses? Why do you want more of men and less of God? (p. 287).

2. More than human words

Certainly we admit gladly that there is a "human side of the Bible—its style, language, composition, history and culture." God used men to write the Bible. But the Bible never puts the emphasis on Scripture as coming from men, and neither should we. The Scriptures are fundamentally the Word of God, not the word of men, except in some incidental and controlled and limited sense. And that human side is wholly secondary, and is treated as incidental when the Bible speaks of itself, its origin and authority (p. 141).

3. Sovereign superintendence

The circumstances of the Bible writers? God prepared them. The heart-attitude and emotions of the writers? God arranged that, too. And the vocabularies, the style, the idiosyncracies of various writers? Yes, God planned all that so that each one was chosen before he was born and fitted to be the instrument God wanted to use. The varying styles are all God's styles in the Bible. God made the men and made the styles, and used them according to plan (p. 206).

Were the epistles written by the Apostle Paul formed in the matrix of his own customary manner of speech? Is the style in the epistles distinctively Paul's usual style? There is reason to doubt it. Christians at Corinth did not think that the inspired letters were compatible with his usual manner of speech. In II Corinthians 10:10 Paul reports what they said: "For his letters, they say, are weighty and powerful; but his bodily presence is weak, and his speech contemptible" (p. 143).

We do not have other uninspired writings by Bible authors so we cannot say just how much the styles used are distinctive of the writers, but we believe God prepared the individuals so that their style, vocabulary and viewpoints, as much as they are included in the Scriptures, are exactly in God's plan (p. 136).

II. The Nature of Scripture

A. *The Word of God*

The Bible does not simply in some places "contain the Word of God"; the Bible *is* the Word of God (p. 88, italics his).

The perfect Word of God is all perfect. It is all the Word of God. All of it is settled forever in Heaven (Ps. 119:89). All of it is incorruptible and cannot be broken (1 Peter 1:23; John 10:35) (p. 96).

All of us see that men wrote the Bible and in some secondary sense, we see that the Bible is a book from men. Of course, it is primarily and originally the Word of God and not of men (p. 136).

The Bible is still the Word of God and not the word of men except in some incidental way that God Himself chose to put Scripture in the style of some man He had prepared to write it (p. 150).

B. *Inerrant*

Psalm 19:7 says, "The law of the Lord is perfect, converting the soul." "The law" originally meant the Pentateuch, the law of Moses. Eventually the term seemed to refer to all the Bible. And here the claim is not simply that the law is good but that it is perfect and that it works the miraculous change of regeneration in the believing heart (p. 64).

The Bible is not necessarily a book of science in the sense of modern terminology and modern theories; it is, however, absolutely correct when it speaks on matters of history or geography (p. 88).

C. *Infallible*

The original autographs of the Scriptures were infallibly correct. "Every word of God is pure" (Prov. 30:5). If one has problems in explaining everything in the Bible, one would have far more problems explaining Christ and Christianity and the Word of God itself mixed with human errors and unreliable statements (p. 88).

If the Bible is not God's own infallible Word, Jesus is not God. So if you lose the Bible you lose Christianity and salvation. Again we say, Christ and the Bible stand or fall together (p. 128).

III. Criticism of Scripture

Higher criticism tends to sit in judgment on the Bible and let poor, sinning, frail, ignorant, mortal men pass judgment on the Word of God (p. 136).

Summary

According to the fundamentalist view of John R. Rice, the Bible is verbally dictated (word-for-word) from God to the biblical writers, who were secretaries of the Holy Spirit. Hence, the Bible is God's infallible and inerrant words. There is a human element to

Scripture, though there are no human sources. The human side of Scripture is in the vocabularies and styles of the writers. These vocabularies and styles were, however, providentially formed by God in advance so that by advanced planning God chose the very words and style that He would breathe out through men in recording the Scriptures. As a result, the Bible is as perfect as God is. To attribute any flaw to Scripture by biblical criticism is to exalt man's fallible reason over God's infallible Word.

8

The Neoorthodox View of the Bible

Neoorthodoxy, or neoreformation theology, may be understood as a reaction against
liberalism, but also as a refusal to return to an orthodox
view of the Bible. Two well-known representatives of
this view are Karl Barth and Emil Brunner.

Karl Barth (1886–1968)

I. The Origin of Scripture

A. *God the Source of the Bible*

Certainly it is not our faith which makes the Bible the
Word of God. . . . That the Bible is the Word of God
is not left to accident or to the course of history and to
our self-will, but to the God of Abraham, Isaac and
Jacob (Karl Barth, *Church Dogmatics*, 2 vols., ed. G.
W. Bromiley [New York: Charles Scribner's Sons,
1936], 1:534).

B. *The Bible Not Identical to the Word of God*

The statement that the Bible is the Word of God cannot therefore say that the Word of God is tied to the Bible. On the contrary, what it must say is that the Bible is tied to the Word of God (ibid., 1:513).

C. *The Conveying of the Bible in the Word of God*

"It holdeth God's word," is what Luther once said about the Bible. . . . It only "holds," encloses, limits and surrounds it: that is the indirectness of the identity of revelation and the Bible (ibid., 1:492).

D. *The Bible as One Form of the Threefold Word of God*

This is primarily because apart from Jesus Christ Himself there is still this other form of the Word of God, which Scripture needs to be the Word of God, just as it needs Scripture. Preaching and the sacrament of the Church do indeed need the basis and authority and authenticity of the original Word of God in Scripture to be the Word of God (ibid., 1:501).

E. *The Purpose of the Bible*

[The human words] are the instruments by which [the Bible] aims at becoming a Word which is apprehended by men and therefore a Word which justifies and sanctifies men, by which it aims at executing upon men the grace of God which is its content (ibid., 1:223).

II. The Nature of Scripture

A. *A Record of Revelation*

1. In signs

   In every age, therefore, the Evangelical decision will have to be a decision for Holy Scripture as such. As such, of course, it is only a sign. Indeed, it is the sign of a sign, i.e., of the prophetic-apostolic witness of revelation as the primary sign of Jesus Christ (ibid., 1:583).

2. In events

Among the signs of the objective reality of revelation we have to understand certain definite events and relations and orders within the world in which revelation is an objective reality, and therefore within the world which is also our world, the world of our nature and history (ibid., 1:223).

To say "the Word of God" is to say the work of God. It is not to contemplate a state or fact but to watch an event, and an event which is relevant to us, an event which is an act of God, an act of God which rests on a free decision (ibid., 1:527).

B. *A Witness to the Word of God*

"What stands there," in the pages of the Bible, is the witness to the *Word of God*, the Word of God in this testimony of the Bible. Just how far it stands there, however, is a fact that demands unceasing discovery, interpretation, and recognition (Karl Barth, *Evangelical Theology: An Introduction,* trans. G. Folley [New York: Holt, Rinehart and Winston, 1963], p. 36, italics his).

In contrast to all kinds of similar literature these communities approved the canon as the original and faithful document of what the witnesses of the resurrection saw, heard, and proclaimed. They were the first to acknowledge this collection as genuine and authoritative testimony to the one Word of God, at the same time taking over, with a remarkable naturalness and ease, the Old Testament canon from the synagogue (ibid., p. 30).

C. *Errant*

1. Contradictions

   There are obvious overlappings and contradictions—e.g., between the Law and the prophets,
   between John and the Synoptists, between Paul
   and James (*Dogmatics*, 1:2.509).

2. Cultural accommodations

   Each [biblical author] in his own way and degree,
   they [*sic*] shared the culture of their age and envi-
   ronment. . . . Instead of talking about the "errors"
   of the biblical authors in this sphere, if we want to
   go to the heart of things it is better to speak only
   about their "capacity for errors." For in the last
   resort even in relation to the general view of the
   world and man the insight and knowledge of our
   age can be neither divine nor even Solomonic
   (ibid., 1:2.508–9).

3. Scientifically fallible

   The post-Biblical theologian may, no doubt, possess a better astronomy, geography, zoology, psychology, physiology, and so on than these biblical
   witnesses possessed; but as for the Word of God,
   he is not justified in comporting himself in relationship to those witnesses as though he knew
   more about the Word than they (*Theology*, p. 31).

4. Higher criticism

   [Higher criticism] migrates from the Old Testament to the New and returns again, from the
   Yahwist to the priestly codex, from the psalms of
   David to the proverbs of Solomon, from the Gospel of John to the synoptic gospels, from the Letter
   to the Galatians to the so-called "straw" epistle of
   James, and so on continually. Within all of these

writings the pilgrimage leads from one level of tradition to another, taking into account every stage of tradition that may be present or surmised. In this respect the work of theology might be compared to the task of circling a high mountain which, although it is one and the same mountain, exists and manifests itself in very different shapes (ibid., p. 34).

D. *Fallible*

The prophets and apostles as such . . . were real, historical men as we are, and therefore sinful in their action, and capable and actually guilty of error in their spoken and written word (*Dogmatics*, 1:2.529).

But the vulnerability of the Bible, i.e., its capacity for error, also extends to its religious or theological content (ibid., 1:509).

EMIL BRUNNER (1889–1966)

I. The Origin of Scripture

A. *The Word of God*

There is a certain danger in this assumption that the "Word of God" can be equated with Holy Scripture. This view arose from a twofold misunderstanding: first, from an academic view of the nature of revelation; secondly, from a Judaistic understanding of the Bible. The Bible itself does not give any occasion for this misunderstanding; by "revelation" it does not mean a supernaturally revealed doctrine; nor does it equate "revelation" either with a collection of books or with one particular Book; in the Bible "revelation" means God's mighty acts for man's salvation (Emil Brunner, *Revelation and Reason*, trans. O. Wyon [Philadelphia: Westminster, 1946], p. 118).

The content of Scripture is true, not because as a

whole it is to be regarded as God's word, but because and to the extent that God meets me there and speaks: He attests Himself to me as present and "decides me": that is why we call Scripture the Word of God (Emil Brunner, *The Word of God and Modern Man,* trans. D. Cairns [Richmond: John Knox, 1964], p. 32).

B. *The Word of Man*

The word of Scripture is not in itself the word of God but of man, just as the historical appearance of the God-man is in itself that of a man (ibid.).

II. The Nature of Scripture

A. *Authoritative*

1. An instrumental authority

   Scripture is not a *formal* authority which demands belief in all it contains from the outset, but it is an *instrumental* authority, in so far as it contains that element before which I must bow in the truth, which also itself awakens in men the certainty of truth. This is what Luther means by the "Word of God," which therefore is not identical with the Word of Scripture, although it is only given to me through the Scriptures, and as the Word of the Scriptures. . . . Thus the content and the real authority of Scripture is Christ (Emil Brunner, *The Christian Doctrine of God,* trans. O. Wyon [London: Lutterworth, 1949], p. 110, italics his).

2. A derived authority

   As in the case of the Reformers, we must express our first principle thus: the Scriptures have the authority of a norm, and the basis for this principle is this: the Scriptures possess this authority because they are the *primary witness* to the revelation of God in Jesus Christ (ibid., p. 45, italics his).

> We believe in Christ, not because Scripture, or the Apostles, teach us about Him in such and such a way, but we believe in the Scriptures because, and in so far as they teach Christ. The authority of Scripture is not formal but material: Christ, the revelation (ibid., p. 110).

3. A subjective authority

> The word in Scripture, Christ, becomes the same as the word in the heart, the Holy Spirit (*God and Man*, p. 28).

> Faith in Jesus Christ is not based upon a previous faith in the Bible, but it is based solely upon the witness of the Holy Spirit; this witness, however, does not come to us save through the witness of the Apostles—that apostolic testimony to which our relation is one of freedom, and, although it is true, it is fundamental for us, it is in no way dogmatically binding, in the sense of the theory of Verbal Inspiration (*Doctrine of God*, p. 34).

B. *Cultural Accommodations*

> The orthodox view of the Bible . . . is an absolutely hopeless state of affairs. . . . God's revelation cannot be measured by the yardstick of theological doctrine. It has pleased God to make use of childlike and primitive ideas as an expression of His will (*Revelation and Reason*, p. 291).

C. *Errant and Fallible*

1. Contradictions

> For at some points the variety of the Apostolic doctrine . . . is an irreconcilable contradiction. In spite of this, even the Epistle of James contributes something to our knowledge of Christ that we should not gain from Paul alone, and which, . . . acts as a corrective (ibid., p. 290).

Literary criticism of the Bible brought to light the thousands of contradictions and human characteristics with which the Old and New Testaments abound. In this way the authority of the Bible was completely overthrown (*God and Man*, p. 36).

2. Scientifically inaccurate

This truth is that the Holy Scriptures contain no divine oracles about all kinds of possible cosmological facts (*Revelation and Reason*, p. 280).

In so far as the Bible speaks about subjects of secular knowledge, it has no teaching authority. Neither its astronomical, cosmological picture of the world, nor its geographical view, nor its zoological, ethnographical or historical statements are binding upon us, whether they are in the Old Testament or in the New. Here, rather, free course should be given to rational scientific criticism (*Doctrine of God*, p. 48).

Fundamentally, Karl Barth's *Dogmatik* takes the same position: "The Bible is not a book of sacred oracles; it is not an organ of direct communication. It is real witness" (I, 2, p. 562). He says that we could not expect that the Apostles and Prophets, in addition to their encounter with the divine revelation, "should also have had imparted to them a compendium of . . . divine Wisdom concerning everything in the universe . . ." (op. cit., p. 564) (ibid., p. 113).

D. *A Record of Revelation*

1. In doctrine

Orthodoxy, which understands revelation as revealed doctrine, finds it very easy to establish correct doctrine. All one has to do is to formulate the revealed doctrine—in a formal sense—for purposes of instruction, in a systematic or catechetical form. The doctrine is already there, in the revelation. We find it impossible to take this enviable short-cut; but we are also aware at what a price this short-cut was purchased, what terrible consequences sprang from it, and indeed, that these consequences are still bearing their own fruit (*Doctrine of God,* p. 28).

2. In an event

   There is no such thing as revelation-in-itself, because revelation consists always of the fact that something is revealed to *me*. Revelation is . . . an act of God, an event involving two parties; it is a personal address (*God and Man,* p. 32, italics his).

3. In a person

   Between us and the Old Testament, however, there stands a new form of revelation, the fulfilment of all that was only promised in the Old Testament, and the actual content of the divine revelation proclaimed by the Apostles and the Church: Jesus Christ Himself. Thus this "revelation" is not a "Word" but a Person—a human life fully visible within history, a human destiny so like, and so unlike, every other: Jesus of Nazareth (*Doctrine of God,* p. 23).

   Therefore "I am the Truth." This is not an impersonal, objective "it" truth, but a "Thou" truth. In this Event of revelation, in the Person of Christ, the divine Thou addresses me, in love. God imparts Himself to me in the life of Him who alone was able to say [this] (*Revelation and Reason,* p. 370).

E. *Verbal Inspiration*

   As a matter of fact, however, this doctrine of revelation [verbal inspiration] proved to be the death of faith, and the dogma of inspiration the very point on which orthodoxy quickly and finally came to an end (*God and Man*, p. 36).

The doctrine of the verbal inspiration of Holy Scripture . . . cannot be regarded as an adequate formulation of the authority of the Bible. It is a product of . . . late Judaism, not of Christianity. The Apostolic writings never claim for themselves a verbal inspiration of this kind, with the infallibility which it implies (*Revelation and Reason*, pp. 127–28).

Once the fatal step is taken of regarding Scripture as true in itself, it is obvious that this quality applies equally to every single part of Scripture down to the smallest detail. . . . The dogma of verbal inspiration is involved not as the cause but as the consequence of the new unspiritual conception. The identity of the word of Scripture with the word of God has now changed from indirect to direct (*God and Man*, p. 34).

III. The Historical Development of Verbal Inspiration

A. *The Position of Judaism and Early Christianity*

From the very beginning the Christian Church possessed a Sacred Scripture which had absolute canonical authority: the Old Testament. Its authority was based upon the fact that it was the work of the Holy Spirit (2 Tim. 3:16). The doctrine of Verbal Inspiration was already known to pre-Christian Judaism . . . and was probably also taken over by Paul and the rest of the Apostles (*Doctrine of God*, p. 107).

B. *The Position of Martin Luther*

In spite of the fact that [Luther] could fight Rome with the Scriptures only, not only did he not (like the "orthodox" of a later date) set up a doctrine of Verbal

Inspiration, and thus of the Infallibility of the Text of the Bible, but, going further than any previous critical views of Scripture, he made a distinction between Scriptures that were "canonical" and those which were not (not in the sense of being included in the Canon or not, but in the sense that some were binding and others were not) (ibid., p. 109).

C. *The Position of John Calvin*

Calvin is already moving away from Luther toward the doctrine of Verbal Inspiration. His *doctrine* of the Bible is entirely the traditional, formally authoritative view (ibid., p. 111, italics his).

D. *The Position From Post-Reformation to Modern Times*

From the end of the sixteenth century onwards there was no other "principle of Scripture" than this formal authoritarian one. Whatever development took place after this culminated in the most strict and most carefully formulated doctrine of Verbal Inspiration which is characteristic of orthodoxy proper— Lutheran as well as Reformed (ibid.).

E. *The Modern Position*

The orthodox doctrine of Verbal Inspiration has been finally destroyed. It is clear that there is no connection between it and scientific research and honesty: we are forced to make a decision for or against this view (Emil Brunner, *The Mediator*, trans. O. Wyon [Philadelphia: Westminster, 1947], p. 105).

IV. Criticism of Scripture

A. *Authenticity*

The written word, which was handed down to us as "Apostolic," was not intended to be regarded as fixed, once for all, in this written form, and therefore of particular importance, but it was meant as a substitute for the oral word of the Apostles, just as a letter is a substitute for a personal meeting (*Revelation and Reason*, p. 126).

B. *Historicity*

1. The Old Testament

With the elimination of the historical element from the story of the "primitive state" a certain deterministic burden of dogmatic conceptions has been removed (ibid., p. 280).

The labors of scientific historical critics—and this should be openly acknowledged—have given us the Prophets of Israel anew. Similarly, the psalms, which were to a large extent unintelligible while it was supposed that they were all written by David, have revealed new depths of meaning since they have been severed from this pseudonymous authorship (ibid., p. 287).

2. The New Testament

So we perceive that the labors of historical critics are . . . a help for the right understanding of the Word of God. Historical criticism certainly destroys a good deal, but it destroys nothing of the truth of God. . . . Thanks to the work of the critics we have gained the possibility of a far fuller understanding of the message of the Apostles and the Prophets (ibid., p. 292).

Jesus Himself gave His teaching as Matthew, Mark, and Luke record it, and not as it is recorded by John (ibid., p. 288).

It [historical criticism] has pointed out various contradictions in the books of Acts, and has discovered various inconsistencies in the assignment of certain definite writings to well-known Apostles as their authors (ibid., p. 285).

Summary

Neoorthodoxy rejects the orthodox view of an infallible and inerrant Bible. The Bible is not a propositional revelation; revelation is personal. Instead, the Bible *witnesses* to and *records* God's revelation in the person of Christ. The Bible is not the Word of God but becomes the Word of God to us when we meet Christ through it. Barth admits the possibility of errors in Scripture; Brunner acknowledges thousands of them. Both believe, however, that God speaks through the Bible as an *instrument* of His revelation. They acknowledge but reject the historic orthodox view that the Bible has formal authority; they accept it as a book with instrumental authority insofar as it reveals Christ to us.

9

The Liberal-Evangelical View of the Bible

THERE IS A view of Scripture that is neither orthodox nor neoorthodox. It is neither liberal nor evangelical. Since it combines elements of both views, it seems fitting to call it liberal-evangelical. Whatever name one gives to the view, the most notable proponent of it is C. S. Lewis. In addition to his popularity on other topics, the uniqueness of his view warrants a special treatment here.

I. The Origin of Scripture

A. *The Voice of God*

Certainly it seems to me that from having had to reach what is really the Voice of God in the cursing Psalms through all the horrible distortions of the human medium, I have gained something I might not have gained from a flawless, ethical exposition (C. S. Lewis, *Reflections on the Psalms* [New York: Harcourt, Brace, 1958], p. 114).

91

Though hideously distorted by the human instrument, something of the Divine voice can be heard in
these passages (ibid., p. 32).

B. *Conveyed Through Humans*

1. A divine taking-up of literature

   For we are taught that the Incarnation itself proceeded "not by the conversion of the godhead into
   flesh, but by taking of [the] manhood into God";
   in it human life becomes the vehicle of Divine life.
   If the Scriptures proceed not by conversion of
   God's word into a literature but by taking up of a
   literature to be the vehicle of God's word, this is
   not anomalous (ibid., p. 116).

2. The literary vehicle

   If the Old Testament is a literature thus "taken
   up," made the vehicle of what is more than
   human, we can of course set no limit to the weight
   or multiplicity of meanings which may have been
   laid upon it. If any writer may say more than he
   knows and mean more than he meant, then these
   writers will be especially likely to do so. And not
   by accident (ibid., p. 117).

3. Divine-human conflicts

   We read [about] the whole Jewish experience of
   God's gradual and graded self-revelation [so as] to
   feel the very contentions between the Word and
   the human material through which it works (ibid.,
   p. 114).

4. Divine superintendence

   I take it that the whole Old Testament consists of
   the same sort of material as any other literature—
   chronicle (some of it obviously pretty accurate),
   poems, moral and political diatribes, romances,

and what not; but all taken into the service of God's word. Not all, I suppose, in the same way. There are prophets who write with the clearest awareness that Divine compulsion is upon them. There are chroniclers whose intention may have been merely to record. There are poets like those in the Song of Songs who probably never dreamed of any but a secular and natural purpose in what they composed. There is (and it is no less important) the work first of the Jewish and then of the Christian Church in preserving and canonizing just these books. There is the work of redactors and editors in modifying them. On all of these I suppose a Divine pressure; of which not by any means all need have been conscious (ibid., p. 111).

II. The Nature of Scripture

A. *Authority*

Whatever view we hold of the divine authority of Scripture must make room for the following facts.

1. The distinction which St. Paul makes in 1 Cor vii between [not I but the Lord] (v. 10) and [I speak, not the Lord] (v. 12).

2. The apparent inconsistencies between the genealogies in Matt i and Luke iii; with the accounts of the death of Judas in Matt xxvii. 5 and Acts i.18–19.

3. St. Luke's own account of how he obtained his matter (i. 1–4).

4. The universally admitted unhistoricity (I do not say, of course, falsity) of at least some narratives in Scripture (the parables), which may well extend also to Jonah and Job.

5. If every good and perfect gift comes from the Father of lights then all true and edifying writings, whether in Scripture or not, must be *in some sense* inspired [italics his].

6. Inspiration may operate in a wicked man without his knowing it, and he can then utter the untruth he intends . . . as well as truth he does not intend. (See John 11:49–52) (Cited in M. J. Christensen, *C. S. Lewis on Scripture* [Waco: Word, 1979], pp. 98–99).

B. *Fallibility*

   1. General statement

      Some people find the miraculous so hard to believe that they cannot imagine any reason for my acceptance of it other than a prior belief that every sentence of the Old Testament has historical or scientific truth. But this I do not hold, any more than St. Jerome did when he said that Moses described Creation "after the manner of a popular poet" (as we should say, mythically) or than Calvin did when he doubted whether the story of Job were history or fiction (Lewis, *The Psalms*, p. 109).

   2. Myths

      a. *Adam and Eve*

         What exactly happened when Man fell, we do not know; but if it is legitimate to guess, I offer the following picture—a "myth" in the Socratic sense,[1] a not unlikely tale.

         For all I can see, it might have concerned the

---

[1]I.e., an account of what *may have been* the historical fact. Not to be confused with "myth" in Dr. Niebuhr's sense (i.e., a symbolical representation of nonhistorical truth) (ibid., p. 64, italics his).

literal eating of a fruit, but the question is of no consequence (ibid., p. 68).

b. *Job*

The *Book of Job* appears to me unhistorical because it begins about a man quite unconnected with all history or even legend, with no genealogy, living in a country of which the Bible elsewhere has hardly anything to say; because . . . the author quite obviously writes as a story-teller not as a chronicler (ibid., p. 110).

c. *Jonah*

The question about Jonah and the great fish does not turn simply on intrinsic probability. The point is that the whole *Book of Jonah* has to me the air of being a moral romance, a quite different kind of thing from, say the account of King David or the New Testament narratives, not pegged like them into any historical situation.

In what sense does the Bible "present" the Jonah story "as historical"? Of course, it doesn't say "This is fiction," but then neither does our Lord say that the Unjust Judge, Good Samaritan, or Prodigal Son are fiction. (I would put *Esther* in the same category as *Jonah* for the same reason.) (Christensen, *Lewis on Scripture*, pp. 96–97).

C. *Errancy*

1. Historical limitations

It seems to me that 2 and 4 [in II. A above] rule out the view that every statement in Scripture must be *historical* truth. And 1, 3, 5, and 6 rule out the view that inspiration is a single thing in the sense that, if present at all, it is always present in the same mode and the same degree. Therefore, I think, rule out the view that any one passage taken in isolation can be assumed to be inerrant in exactly the same sense as any other: e.g., that the numbers of O.T. armies (which in view of the size of the country, if true, involve continuous miracle) are statistically correct. That the overall operation of Scripture is to convey God's Word to the reader (he also needs his inspiration) who reads it in the right spirit, I fully believe. That it *also* gives true answers to all the questions (often religiously irrelevant) which he might ask, I don't. The very kind of truth we are often demanding was, in my opinion, not even envisaged by the ancients (ibid., p. 199, italics his).

2. Errors and contradictions

The human qualities of the raw materials show through. Naivety, error, contradiction, even (as in the cursing Psalms) wickedness are not removed. The total result is not "the Word of God" in the sense that every passage, in itself, gives impeccable science or history (Lewis, *The Psalms*, pp. 111–12).

3. Antireligious portions

Nor would I (now) willingly spare from my Bible something in itself so anti-religious as the nihilism of Ecclesiastes. We get there a clear, cold picture of man's life without God. That statement is itself part of God's word (ibid., p. 115).

We shall find in the Psalms expressions of a cruelty more vindictive and a self-righteousness more complete than anything in the classics. If we ignore such passages and read only a few selected favourite Psalms, we miss the point. For the point is precisely this: that these same fanatic and homicidal Hebrews, and not the more enlightened peoples, again and again—for brief moments—reach a Christian level of spirituality (C. S. Lewis, *Christian Reflections* [Grand Rapids: Eerdmans, 1974], p. 116).

One way of dealing with these terrible or (dare we say?) contemptible Psalms is simply to leave them alone. But unfortunately the bad parts will not "come away clean"; they may, as we have noticed, be intertwined with the most exquisite things (Lewis, *The Psalms*, pp. 21–22).

It is monstrously simple-minded to read the cursings in the Psalms with no feeling except one of horror at the uncharity of the poets. They are indeed devilish (ibid., p. 25).

Let God always remember against him the sins of his parents. Even more devilish in one verse is the, otherwise beautiful, 137 where a blessing is pronounced on anyone who will snatch up a Babylonian baby and beat its brains out against the pavement (ibid., pp. 20–21).

D. *Inspiration: Orthodox View Rejected*

One can respect, and at moments envy, both the Fundamentalist's view of the Bible and the Roman Catholic's view of the Church. But there is one argument which we should beware of using for either position: God must have done what is best, this is best, therefore God has done this. For we are mortals and do not know what is best for us, and it is dangerous to prescribe what God must have done—especially when we cannot for the life of us, see that He has after all done it (ibid., p. 112).

III. Criticism of Scripture

A. *Authorship of Psalms*

How old the Psalms, as we now have them, really are is a question for the scholars. I am told there is one (No. 18) which might really have come down from the age of David himself; that is, from the tenth century B.C. Most of them, however, are said to be "post exilic"; the book was put together when the Hebrews, long exiled in Babylonia, were repatriated by that enlightened ruler, Cyrus of Persia. This would bring us down to the sixth century. How much earlier material the book took in is uncertain (Lewis, *Christian Reflections*, p. 114).

B. *Historicity*

1. Creation account

I have therefore no difficulty in accepting, say, the view of those scholars who tell us that the account of Creation in *Genesis* is derived from earlier Semitic stories which were Pagan and mythical (Lewis, *The Psalms*, p. 110).

2. Old Testament miracles

A consideration of the Old Testament miracles is beyond the scope of this book and would require many kinds of knowledge which I do not possess. My present view—which is tentative and liable to any amount of correction—would be that just as, on the factual side, a long preparation culminates in God's becoming incarnate as Man, so, on the documentary side, truth first appears in mythical form and then by a long process of condensing or focussing finally becomes incarnate as History. This involves the belief that Myth in general is not merely misunderstood history (as Euhemerus thought) nor diabolical illusion (as some of the

Fathers thought) nor priestly lying (as the philosophers of the Enlightenment thought) but, at its best, a real though unfocussed gleam of divine truth falling on human imagination. The Hebrews, like other people, had mythology: but as they were the chosen people so their mythology was the chosen mythology—the mythology chosen by God to be the vehicle of the earliest sacred truths, the first step in that process which ends in the New Testament where truth has become completely historical. Whether we can ever say with certainty where, in this process of crystalisation, any particular Old Testament story falls, is another matter. I take it that the memoirs of David's court come at one end of the scale and are scarcely less historical than St. Mark or Acts; and that the Book of Jonah is at the opposite end (C. S. Lewis, *Miracles* [New York: Macmillan, 1963], p. 139, n.l.).

3. Biblical events

[The resurrection of Christ is a historical and very important event], but the value of others (e.g., the fate of Lot's wife) hardly at all. And the ones, whose historicity matters, are, as God's will, those where it is plain (C. S. Kilby, *The Christian World of C. S. Lewis* [Grand Rapids: Eerdmans, 1964], p. 153).

A theology which denies the historicity of nearly everything in the Gospels to which Christian life and affections and thought have been fastened for nearly two millennia—which, either denies the miraculous altogether or, more strangely, after swallowing the camel of the Resurrection strains at such gnats as the feeding of the multitudes—if offered to the uneducated man can produce only one or other of two effects. It will make him a

Roman Catholic or an atheist (Lewis, *Christian Reflections*, p. 153).

C. *Textual Criticism*

We are not fundamentalists. We think that different elements in this sort of theology have different degrees of strength. The nearer it sticks to mere textual criticism, of the old sort, Lachmann's sort, the more we are disposed to believe in it (ibid., p. 163).

IV. The Bible and Science

A. *Theistic Evolution*

For long centuries God perfected the animal form which was to become the vehicle of humanity and the image of Himself (Lewis, *The Psalms*, p. 65).

The creature may have existed for ages in this stage before it became man: it may even have been clever enough to make things which a modern archaeologist would accept as proof of its humanity. But it was only an animal because all its physical and psychical processes were directed to purely material and natural ends. Then, in the fullness of time, God caused to descend upon this organism, both on its psychology and physiology, a new kind of consciousness which could say "I" and "me," which could look upon itself as an object, which knew God, which could make judgments of truth, beauty, and goodness, and which was so far above time that it could perceive time flowing past (ibid.).

B. *The Creation Myth*

When a series of such re-telling turns a creation story which at first had almost no religious or metaphysical significance into a story which achieves the idea of true Creation and of a transcendent Creator (as *Genesis* does), then nothing will make me believe that some of the re-tellers, or some one of them, has not been guided by God.

Thus something originally merely natural—the kind of myth that is found among most nations—will have been raised by God above itself, qualified by Him and compelled by Him to serve purposes which of itself it would not have served (ibid., p. 110).

V. Interpretation of the Scriptures

A. *Exegetical Rules*

I suggest two rules for exegetics: 1) Never take the images literally. 2) When the *purport* of the images—what they say to our fear and hope and will and affections—seems to conflict with the theological abstractions, trust the purport of the images every time. For our abstract thinking is itself a tissue of analogies: a continual modelling of spiritual reality in legal or chemical or mechanical terms (C. S. Lewis, *Letters to Malcolm: Chiefly on Prayer* [New York: Harcourt, Brace & World, 1963–64], p. 52, italics his).

B. *Theological Abstractions*

I know this language is analogical. But when we say that, we must not smuggle in the idea that we can throw the analogy away and, as it were, get in behind it to a purely literal truth. All we can really substitute for the analogical expression is some theological abstraction (ibid., p. 51).

C. *Experiences*

This is the most remarkable of the powers of Poetical language: to convey to us the quality of experiences which we have not had, or perhaps can never have, to use factors within our experience—as two or more roads on a map show us where a town that is off the map must lie (Lewis, *Christian Reflections*, p. 133).

The very essence of our life as conscious beings, all
day and every day, consists of something which cannot be communicated except by hints, similes,
metaphors, and the use of those emotions (themselves not very important) which are pointers to it
(ibid., p. 140).

Summary

Lewis holds many things in common with the liberal
view of Scripture: (1) There are some errors and contradictions in the Bible; (2) some of it is myth, not fact;
(3) some stories are not historical; and (4) the Creation
account is not to be taken as scientifically true. On the
other hand, Lewis criticizes those who reject the historicity of the life, teachings, and resurrection of Christ.
Further, he believes God took the human words of
Scripture and "elevated" them so that they convey the
voice of God.

10

The Neoevangelical View of the Bible

THIS VIEW MAY also be called the neo-Reformed view, since it comes mainly from theologians in the Reformed tradition. But inasmuch as some Evangelicals have adopted this or a similar view, it seems best to call it neoevangelical. The most important proponent of this view is the Dutch theologian G. C. Berkouwer. The American theologian Jack Rogers, of Fuller Seminary, holds substantially the same view.

G. C. BERKOUWER (1903–)

I. The Origin of Scripture

A. *The Word of God*

1. And the word of man

We have frequently come across the characterization of Scripture as the Word of God and the word of men. Reliability, of course, was always discussed in direct relationship to this, particularly in view of the truly human aspect of Scripture. We do not merely have in mind the general consideration that error belongs to human nature. We have in mind above all the contrast noted frequently in Scripture between the Word of God and the words of men, between relying on God and relying on man (p. 240). (All quotations are from G. C. Berkouwer, *Holy Scripture: Studies in Dogmatics* [Grand Rapids: Eerdmans, 1975].)

2. A confession

This "is" is not a postulate of our longings for certainty which cannot withstand the assaults of the human. Rather, it is truly a *confession* that continues to be filled with expectation in listening to the many voices within the one voice in this Scripture (p. 168, italics his).

3. Nonsupernatural

This can be understood if one does not initially misunderstand the glory of God and does not wish to interpret the God-breathed character in an abstract supernaturalistic and "miraculous" manner (p. 170).

B. *Conveyed Through Humans*

1. Divine sovereignty

In reading Scripture we encounter some of the questions aroused in men related to . . . becoming bearers of God's Word. Moses does not deem himself "eloquent" (Ex. 4:10), and Isaiah exclaims "Woe is me" because he is a man of unclean lips (Isa. 6:5). . . . This divine taking-into-service has an aspect of triumph and sovereignty, yet it does not erase the weakness of the human word nor its limitations. Time and again we note a vivid awareness of God's using weak human "instruments" (p. 206).

The speech of men in prophecy is the way of the reliable testimony of God (p. 146).

2. Human limitations

It is explicitly referred to in Bavinck's words: "Christ became flesh, a servant without form or comeliness, the most despised among men . . . and so also the Word, the revelation of God entered creation, in the life and history of men and people in every form of dream and vision, of research and meditation, even as far as the humanly weak and ignoble; the Word became Scripture and as Scripture subjected itself to the fate of all writing" (p. 199).

Fundamentalism greatly obscures the contexts in which God himself gave us Scripture. Back of fundamentalism lies something of an unconscious wish not to have God's Word enter the creaturely realm—or, to use Bavinck's words, "into the humanly weak and despised and base"—and the wish that Scripture should not subject itself "as writing to the fate of all writings" (p. 25).

I believe that I am judging no one unfairly when I say that fundamentalism, in its eagerness to maintain Holy Scripture's divinity, does not fully realize the significance of Holy Scripture as a prophetic-apostolic, and consequently human, testimony (p. 22).

II. The Nature of Scripture

A. *Cultural Accommodations*

But Paul, in contrast, did not in the least render timeless propositions concerning womanhood. Rather, he wrote various testimonies and prescriptions applicable to particular—and to a certain degree transparent—situations against a background of specific morals and customs of that period. This realization has increasingly penetrated even to areas where there has been no hesitation to affirm Scripture as the Word of God (p. 187).

Ramm wrote rightly . . . that the Holy Spirit "did not give to the writers the secrets of modern science." Various excessive examples (including even nuclear theories) are in his opinion "a misunderstanding of the nature of inspiration." They do not take into account that Scripture came to us "in terms of the culture in which the writers wrote" (p. 189).

The problem of the God-breathed character of Scripture and continuity gained renewed interest in its connection with the author's level of knowledge in a certain period (Ex. 20:4, Ps. 24:2, [3, Eng. text]; 2 Sam. 22:8; Ps. 136:6; Job 26:5; Ps. 46:3 [2, Eng. text]; Ps. 148:4). This does not mean a capitulation to science as an institution opposed to God's Word, with the additional conclusions that Scripture is unreliable and its witness untrustworthy. Rather, it means a greater degree of naturalness in speaking of Scripture, with a view to its nature and purpose. Corrections of various conceptions of the world—its composition and its place in the universe—are not at all needed then to guarantee the full and clear message of Scripture. Formal problems of correctness (inerrancy alongside infallibility) disintegrate with such a naturalness (p. 182).

B. *Errancy*

   1. Historical limitations

      He who demands that all conceptions occurring in

Scripture be precisely correct on the basis of the God-breathed character of Scripture starts with the presupposition that the voice of God can only then be reliable and that the biblical authors cannot be witnesses and instruments of the God-breathed Scripture when they use certain time-bound conceptions in their writings. This notion of "inerrancy" can quickly lead to the idea that the "correctness" of all these conceptions anticipates later scientific discovery (p. 183).

The concept of error in the sense of incorrectness is obviously being used on the same level as the concept of erring in the sense of sin and deception. The distinction is left rather vague. As a consequence of this, limited historical perception within a certain cultural and scientific situation is, without further stipulation, put on a par with erring in the sense of lying, the opposite of truth. If erring is formalized in such a way, it cannot later be related to truth in a biblical sense, but it continues to function as a formal structure of exactness and correctness. Thus, we are quite far removed from the serious manner with which erring is dealt in Scripture. For there what is meant is not the result of a limited degree of knowledge, but it is a swerving from the truth and upsetting the faith (2 Tim. 2:18) (p. 181).

One will never solve the problem of the Gospels by indiscriminately operating with the concept of "historical reliability," precisely because then one leaves the impression that no further questions need to be answered. As a consequence, all further reflection on this point is subject to suspicion from the start (p. 251).

It was pointed out by many that it was impossible

to write a "biography" of Jesus based on the Gospels, not even by adding up the data from the Gospels so that one would complement another (p. 247).

2. Scientific limitations

This is illustrated in Jan Ridderbos' words: "Moreover Scripture bears the marks of the period and of the milieu in which it was written and it shares in part these marks with the culture which in many ways was interrelated to that of Israel. This is true for writing, language, style, literary genre, ideas, conceptions, world view (cf. the three-decker universe in Ex. 20:4)" (p. 182).

It was pointed out that the authority of Scripture is in no way diminished because an ancient world view occurs in it; for it was not the purpose of Scripture to offer revealing information on that level (p. 181).

3. Myths

Therefore we "cannot directly take up a position against Bultmann's theological concern with demythologizing by means of a text such as 2 Peter 1:16" [from K. H. Schelke, *Die Petrusbriefe* (1961), p. 198]. By "myth" Bultmann does not mean those myths that are rejected as fabrications and are opposed to the truth as *mythoi*. He means rather an imagery connected with a mythical world view. This world view is characterized by the presence of three levels—heaven, earth, and the underworld—so that earth is considered to be the "scene of the supernatural activity of God" [from R. Bultmann, "NT and Mythology" in *Kerygma and Myths*, I, CET (1961), p. 1] (p. 254).

If we are dealing with a penetration of story and

interpretation, should we not accept a creativity of the evangelists from which "fantasy" could be distinguished only with great difficulty? (p. 248).

C. *Inspiration*

1. Organic

We are reminded, by way of background, of what is called—even in catechism books—the transition from a more "mechanical" to a more "organic" view of Scripture. It is clear that this too will determine the nature of one's account (p. 11).

To Bavinck . . . organic inspiration [is] "the unfolding and application of the central fact of revelation, the incarnation of the Word" (p. 199).

2. Not verbal plenary

Burgon is simply forced to give an explanation of "the method of inspiration" regarding the testimony of Scripture: "Every book of it, every chapter of it, every word of it, every syllable of it, every letter of it, is the direct utterance of the Most High." This statement of his disregards all nuances of Scripture (consider the Psalms, Job, Ecclesiastes), as though it were a string of divine or supernaturally revealed statements, ignoring the fact that God's Word has passed through humanity and has incorporated its service (pp. 23–24).

3. Divine intention

At issue is whether and in what way faith is related to the *"gospel* promised *in* Holy Scripture."* Scripture is central because of its nature and intent. For this Scripture is only referred to because its sense and intent is the divine message of salvation (p. 147, italics his).

4. Through human witness

As Ridderbos writes, the evangelists did not intend to give "an historical narrative of Jesus' words and works but a portrayal of Jesus as the Christ." That is the character of our gospel, or, expressed in other terms, not *report* but *witness* (p. 247, italics his).

III. Criticism of Scripture

A. *Not Beyond Criticism*

For various reasons students of Scripture began to wonder more and more whether Holy Scripture as God's Word was truly beyond all criticism as the indubitable *vox Dei*, as a book—however human—of indisputably divine signature (p. 13).

B. *Legitimacy of Biblical Criticism*

Frequently, too little attention is paid to the possibility and legitimacy of biblical research. A supernaturalistic view of revelation would consider any human "research" puzzling and inconceivable (p. 358).

JACK ROGERS (1934–)

I. The Origin of Scripture

A. *Divine Authority*

Evangelicals believe that the Bible is the authoritative word of God (Jack Rogers, ed., *Biblical Authority* [Waco: Word, 1977], p. 17).

B. *Human Authors*

In order to communicate effectively with human beings, God condescended, humbled, and accommodated himself to human categories of thought and speech (Jack Rogers and Donald McKim, *The Author-*

ity and Interpretation of the Bible [New York: Harper & Row, 1979], p. 10).

II. The Nature of Scripture

A. *Organic Inspiration*

The basic interpretative principle of the Reformation had been stated in several ways: the analogy of faith, or Scripture is its own interpreter. The meaning of these phrases was that each part of the Bible was to be understood in relationship to the overall saving message of Scripture. Bavinck attempted to express this relationship of the parts to the whole through the image of the human body. Bavinck's concept, which he called "organic inspiration," drew attention to the fact that there is a center and a periphery to Scripture (Rogers and McKim, *Authority and Interpretation*, p. 391).

B. *Unerring Purpose*

It is no doubt possible to define the meaning of biblical inerrancy according to the Bible's saving purpose and taking into account the human forms through which God condescended to reveal himself (Rogers, *Biblical Authority*, p. 45).

C. *Factually Errant*

It is historically irresponsible to claim that for two thousand years Christians have believed that the authority of the Bible entails a modern concept of inerrancy in scientific and historical details (ibid., p. 44).

To confuse "error" in the sense of technical accuracy with the biblical notion of error as willful deception diverts us from the serious intent of Scripture. The purpose of the Bible is not to substitute for human science. The purpose of the Bible is to warn against human sin and offer us God's salvation in Christ.

Scripture infallibly achieves that purpose. We are called, not to argue Scripture's scientific accuracy, but to accept its saving message (ibid., p. 46).

III. The Purpose of Scripture

A. *Salvation, Not Science*

The last five sections of the Confession dealt especially with how Scripture could be interpreted by a regenerate mind in light of its purpose of bringing us to salvation in Christ. . . . Scripture was not to be used as a source of information in the sciences to refute what the scholars were discovering (ibid., p. 34).

B. *Christ, Not Philosophy*

For the Westminster divines, the final judge in controversies of religion was not just the bare word of Scripture interpreted by human logic, but the Spirit of Christ leading us in Scripture to its central saving witness to him (ibid., p. 35).

IV. Criticism and the Bible

A. *Center Versus Periphery*

By distinguishing between the center and the periphery in Scripture, Kuyper and Bavinck's tradition freed their followers from scholarship and for scholarship. The central saving message of Scripture could be received in faith without waiting for scholarly reasons. The supporting material of Scripture, the human forms of culture and language, were open to scholarly investigation (Rogers and McKim, *Authority and Interpretation*, p. 393).

B. *Purpose Versus Content*

Biblical criticism became a problem, according to Bavinck, only when the critics lost sight of the purpose of Scripture. That purpose, goal, or "destination" of Scripture was "none other than that it should make us wise to salvation." According to Bavinck, Scripture was not meant to give us technically correct scientific information (Rogers, *Biblical Authority,* p. 43).

C. *Inerrant Originals Unprovable*

Thus errorlessness was confined to the original (lost) manuscripts of the Bible. Since the original texts were not available, Warfield seemed to have an unassailable apologetic stance (ibid., p. 39).

V. View of History

A. *Fathers Against Inerrancy*

Augustine, Calvin, Rutherford, and Bavinck, for example, all specifically deny that the Bible should be looked to as an authority in matters of science. To claim them in support of a modern inerrancy theory is to trivialize their central concern that the Bible is our sole authority on salvation and the living of a Christian life (ibid., p. 44).

B. *Old Princeton Theology Wrong*

It is equally irresponsible to claim that the old Princeton theology of Alexander, Hodge, and Warfield is the only legitimate evangelical, or Reformed, theological tradition in America (ibid., p. 45).

Summary

The neoevangelical view differentiates between the Word of God (divine content) and the words of the human authors (human form) of Scripture. The former is infallible, but the latter is not. Hence, the Bible is not infallible divine words but only reliable human words.

The Bible is a human witness to divine revelation. The church *confesses* it as the "Word of God." But the Bible does not express eternal truths about science, history, or even human relations (such as male-female roles). It sees Fundamentalism's view of Scripture as mechanical, verbal dictation. This is rejected in favor of an "organic" inspiration, which admits there are myths and obsolete scientific views reflected in Scripture. The Bible, like all other human books, is subject to mistakes and thus must be judged by biblical (higher) criticism.

Conclusion

On reflection, there are several pertinent questions the Christian needs to consider to determine how he should view the Bible.

1. What, precisely, does the Bible claim about itself? Is God the ultimate Author of Scripture? Does the Bible claim to teach historical and scientific truths? Can the Bible as God's Word err?

2. Did the great fathers of the church agree or disagree with what the Bible claims for itself? What did they teach about the origin and nature of the Bible? Did they believe biblical authority included scientific and historical matters? Did they believe the Bible could err in anything it affirmed? What sort of agreement is there among modern scholars and what the fathers believed?

3. Who was the first person discussed who significantly varied from the biblical and historical position on Scripture? In what ways does his view differ from what the Bible claims for itself?

Which view, then, is right about the origin and nature of the Bible? The orthodox? The liberal? The fundamentalist? The neoorthodox? The liberal-evangelical? Or the neoevangelical? Decide for yourself.

ST. TIMOTHY LUTHERAN CHURCH
4200 MA. KE. STR.Ei
CAMP HILL, rA. 17011